MEMOIRS AND LETTERS

OF

DOLLY MADISON

KENNIKAT PRESS SCHOLARLY REPRINTS
Dr. Ralph Adams Brown, Senior Editor

Series in
AMERICAN HISTORY AND CULTURE
IN THE NINETEENTH CENTURY
Under the General Editorial Supervision of
Dr. Martin L. Fausold
Professor of History, State University of New York

MEMOIRS AND LETTERS

OF

DOLLY MADISON

WIFE OF JAMES MADISON, PRESIDENT
OF THE UNITED STATES

EDITED BY
HER GRAND-NIECE

KENNIKAT PRESS
Port Washington, N. Y./London

MEMOIRS AND LETTERS OF DOLLY MADISON

First published in 1886
Reissued in 1971 by Kennikat Press
Library of Congress Catalog Card No: 70-137922
ISBN 0-8046-1487-3

Manufactured by Taylor Publishing Company   Dallas, Texas

KENNIKAT SERIES ON AMERICAN HISTORY AND
CULTURE IN THE NINETEENTH CENTURY

MEMOIRS AND LETTERS.

CHAPTER I.

In undertaking a little sketch of this nature, I am quite conscious that a relative has peculiar temptations to be partial, — a temper of mind which Mrs. Madison, in the great simplicity of her character, would most cordially have disliked; and therefore, though the skill may be wanting, the endeavor will be to give facts, anecdotes, and letters, as they were handed down by near relatives, privileged to live in her household and enjoy her confidence, suppressing nothing that could interest the many who admire and respect her memory. As those who have seen Mrs. Madison's features and heard her voice are becoming yearly fewer, the number who take an interest in bygone days, and the prominent men and women who fig-

ured in history and society, when our
country was yet in its infancy, is rapidly
increasing; indeed, our great-grandmoth-
ers and grandfathers shape themselves before our eyes, and assume new interest, as
pictures of the life and influences of those
early days are brought before us.

I propose to lay before the public a series of private letters, written, without the
most remote idea of publication, by a woman to her nearest and dearest relations;
and their value consists in the fact, capable of no misconception, that they furnish
an exact transcript of the feelings of the
writer, in times of no ordinary trial.

If it were possible to get at the expression of feelings by women in the heart of
a community more frequently, recorded
in a shape designed to be confidential, it
would serve to present the surest and
most unfailing idea of its general character.

Whether deliberating in the Senate, or
fighting in the field, our strength against
Great Britain was never that of numbers,
nor of wealth, nor of genius; it drew its
nourishment from a more potent source:
from the sentiment that pervaded the

dwellings of the entire population. How much this sentiment did then, and does now, depend upon the character of our women will be too readily understood to require explanation.

The domestic hearth is the scene of the almost exclusive sway of women, and great as the influence thus exercised undoubtedly is, it escapes observation in such manner that history rarely takes much account of it. The maxims of religion, faith, hope, and charity, are instilled by them into the teachings of infancy, thus supplying the only high and pure motives of which mature manhood can, in its subsequent action, ever boast.

John Payne, the grandfather of Mrs. Madison, was an English gentleman of wealth and education, who emigrated to this country and settled on the James River, in the county of Goochland, Virginia. He married Anna Fleming, granddaughter of Sir Thomas Fleming, second son of the Earl of Wigton, of Scotland, and also an emigrant to the Colony, who landed at Jamestown and established himself in Kent County, where he lived until his death.

John Payne the second, the father of Mrs. Madison, left home at an early age to take charge of a plantation in North Carolina given him by his father. He there married Mary Coles, daughter of William Coles, a native of Enniscorthy, Ireland. Her mother, whose maiden name was Philpot, was an aunt of Virginia's orator, Patrick Henry.

The devout believer in the transmission of family qualities will be content with the inheritance of Dolly Madison from this mother and grandmother, both noted for their beauty and popularity. Mary Coles was a great belle, having many admirers, — among them the young Thomas Jefferson, whose promising talents were even then appreciated. In spite, however, of the persistency of friends, John Payne was the favored suitor, and shortly after his marriage purchased an estate in Hanover County, Virginia, within driving distance of Coles Hill, the residence of his father-in-law.

Towards the close of her life, Mrs. Madison frequently recalled the home of her childhood, dwelling upon the great black marble mantelpieces, supported by white

figures. The house was called Scotch-
town because of the emigrants, and was
surrounded by a number of small brick
houses, attached to the main building,
which was very large, having as many as
twenty rooms on a floor.

John Payne was the father of six children, of whom the second is the subject of
this memoir. Much might be said of un-
usual charms discovered by adoring parents during her infancy. Dorothy Payne
first opened her eyes on this world, which
she was destined so thoroughly to enjoy,
on the 20th May, 1768, in North Carolina,
where her parents were visiting; and was
named Dorothy for her mother's aunt,
Mrs. Patrick Henry.

Both father and mother were strict members of the "Society of Friends," and
Dolly's childhood was passed quietly in
their country home until she reached the
age of twelve years. A favorite with all,
she was the particular pet and companion
of her grandmother, who often made her
happy by surreptitious presents of old-
fashioned jewelry, and not daring to wear
them before her father and mother, she
sewed them into a bag, which was tied

around her neck, and concealed beneath her little frock. Almost the first grief of her childhood was the loss of this precious bag, discovered in school, after a long ramble through the woods, during which the string must have become unfastened, scattering the treasure where days of searching proved of no avail.

The cultivation of the female mind at that time was regarded with utter indifference. It may have been that the example of Mrs. Hutchinson in the early Colony days had not yet effaced from the mind of the public a conviction of the danger that may attend the meddling of women with abstruse points of doctrine. And also it was the fashion to ridicule "learned women." The little country school to which Dolly Payne wended her way for the first twelve years was of the simplest description. Reading, writing, and arithmetic were all that was considered necessary, and though her educational advantages were greater after their removal to Philadelphia, her life until she married was rigidly simple and quiet, giving no scope for that intuitive tact and knowledge of character which was so conspicuous in after years.

Equipped with a white linen mask to keep every ray of sunshine from the complexion, a sun-bonnet sewed on her head every morning by her careful mother, and long gloves covering the hands and arms, one can see the prim little figure starting off for school, with books under her arm, and the dear but wicked baubles safely hidden beneath the severely plain Quaker dress.

CHAPTER II.

MR. PAYNE was one of the first of his sect in Virginia to become doubtful — and later conscientiously scrupulous — about the right of slavery. He was called a fanatic, but persisted in his views, selling his plantation and giving freedom to all the slaves. Several of the most devoted servants refused to go, and these he took with him to Philadelphia, whither he moved with his family in 1786, with but one aim in view — the better maintenance of his religious character. There he became an Elder, spoke with great effect at the " Meetings," and was called a Quaker preacher.

Though a strict and particular father, he was also a devoted one, bringing up his children in that religion which has utility for its basis, sending them to schools taught by his own sect, and himself giving them every attention at home. Ornaments and accomplishments were equally forbidden by their religion ; even a clock belonging to an unthinking member was shorn of its beautiful carving by a delegation from the " Meeting," as savoring too much "of the vanities," and in the same systematic way were all the little accomplishments cut off from the children.

Hospitable, generous, and believed to be very rich, as Mr. Payne was, his house became the resort of all needy Southerners, who often took advantage of his liberality. The transition from life on a plantation with many slaves, to town, together with a total ignorance of money matters, brought about an embarrassment in his affairs, and he determined to go into business, taking with him into partnership his eldest son, John, who had been traveling in Europe.

Much of his capital, however, was in Revolutionary money, and as that gradually depreciated in value, he failed, and his family found themselves much reduced in circumstances. This failure had a most depressing effect upon him, physically and mentally, and he never held up his head again, taking to his room, which he left only to be carried to his last resting-place.

All this while the pretty Dolly was

growing in grace and stature, winning
hearts from old and young by the peculiar
charm of manner for which she afterwards
became noted. A tall, slight girl of nine-
teen, with a delicately oval face, and well-
formed, if not perfect, features ; a complexion dazzlingly fair, contrasted with
very black hair ; and blue eyes that gazed
at you with much sweetness, beneath the
modest little Quaker cap. Who knows
what ideal the girl may have had, and why
it was that when the good-looking John
Todd, a promising young lawyer of means,
and a member of the Society of Friends,
proposed to her, the answer was that she
"never meant to marry." Children at that
time, however, were taught to obey their
parents unquestioningly, and when Dolly
was sent for, to the bedside of her father,
and told that he wished her much to become the wife of John Todd, a young man
who had shown him great kindness in his
trouble, and of whom he had the highest
opinion, there was nothing for it but to
obey, which she did with the best possible
grace, and was amply rewarded by seeing
her father tranquil and happy during the
few remaining months of his life, and by

the devotion of a husband who made the three short years of their married life all that could be wished.

In 1792 Lucy Payne, a younger sister of Mrs. Madison, married at fifteen George Steptoe Washington, nephew of General Washington, and then a resident of Jefferson County, Virginia, where he owned a large and valuable property, inherited from his father, Samuel Washington, a gay, fox-hunting squire, who thought much of his wives (of whom he had had five), and his horses and dogs. On the walls of Harewood, I believe, his portrait still hangs, in powdered wig, long coat, and lace ruffles, and by it the likeness of one of his wives, Anne Steptoe, also represented in the elaborate dress of the day, with cushioned hair and blue brocade. Here it was that Mr. Madison came to wed the pretty "Widow Todd."

On the 11th of September, 1793, Mr. Jefferson, then in Philadelphia, wrote to Mr. Morris: "An infectious and deadly fever has broken out in this place. The deaths under it, during the week before last, were about forty, the last week fifty, and this week I fear they will be two hundred, so rapidly is it increasing. Every one is leaving the city who can. Colonel Hamilton has been ill, but on the road to recovery. The President, according to an arrangement made some time ago, left for Mt. Vernon yesterday. The Secretary of War is starting out on a visit to Boston. I shall go in a few days to Virginia. *When* we shall meet again may depend on the course of the malady, and on that may depend the date of my next letter."

Mrs. Todd, with her two children, one a baby of three weeks, was removed in a litter to Gray's Ferry, to avoid the epidemic. Her husband, however, could not be kept away from the infected city, and hurried back, arriving only in time to be present at the death-bed of his father and mother, both victims to the dreadful scourge of yellow fever.

Deaf to the tearful entreaties of his wife, Mr. Todd lingered on in Philadelphia to close his office and give assistance to the many friends needing help. When these duties were over, "he would never leave her again," he said. Alas! a vain boast. He returned to Gray's Ferry, and meeting his mother-in-law, Mrs. Payne, at the door, said, "I feel the fever in my veins, but I must see *her* once more."

Dolly, on hearing his voice, rushed down stairs and threw herself into his arms, heedless of infection, begging to be allowed to go back to town with him.

A few hours afterwards that good, unselfish spirit breathed its last, and the young wife was brought almost to death's door by the fatal scourge.

CHAPTER III.

AFTER a slow recovery, during which time she lost her younger child, Mrs. Todd returned to Philadelphia with her mother and little boy, named after her father, John Payne. All danger of infection was over, but there were many sorrowing hearts, and none more so than this young widow's, bereft of husband and child within a few short days of each other. Still young, only twenty-six, very rich and very attractive, it is only natural that in course of time she should have many admirers ; and one of her friends, a bridesmaid at her wedding, said that "gentlemen would station themselves where they could see her pass," and sometimes she had remonstrated with her, laughingly, " really Dolly, thou must hide thy face, there are so many staring at thee."

It was during one of these walks that Mr. Madison saw Mrs. Todd for the first time, and was so struck with her appearance that he did not rest until an introduction was procured.

Mrs. Lee also tells us of this first meeting, a few days afterwards, when she receives a hurried little note from Dolly, saying, " Dear friend, thou must come to me. Aaron Burr says that the ' great little Madison ' has asked to be brought to see me this evening." She was dressed in a mulberry-colored satin, with a silk tulle kerchief over her neck, and on her head an exquisitely dainty little cap, from which an occasional uncropped curl would escape. In this first interview, at her own house, she captured the heart of the recluse bookworm, Madison, — seventeen years her senior, and always thought to be an irreclaimable old bachelor.

A report soon got about of their engagement ; such unwonted attentions from Mr. Madison excited comment, and rumor was as active in those days as now.

It reached the Presidential mansion, where General and Mrs. Washington were much interested ; and impatient to hear the truth, sent for Mrs. Todd, who all unconscious obeyed the summons at once.

" Dolly," said Mrs. Washington, "is it

true that you are engaged to James Madison?" The fair widow, taken aback, answered stammeringly, "No," she "thought not." "If it is so," Mrs. Washington continued, "do not be ashamed to confess it : rather be proud ; he will make thee a good husband, and all the better for being so much older. We both approve of it ; the esteem and friendship existing between Mr. Madison and my husband is very great, and we would wish thee to be happy." And thus the rumor grew to be an established fact, and in September, 1794, Mrs. Todd left Philadelphia to drive to Harewood, her sister's place in Virginia, where the wedding was to take place. Fortunately the weather was bright and beautiful, as the gay cavalcade were a week on their way : Mrs. Todd in an open barouche, accompanied by her sister, Anna, a child of twelve years, the little boy and a maid ; Mr. Madison and several of their mutual friends driving or riding beside them.

A most delightful picture is given of this country wedding ; friends and neighbors from far and near driving over. Frances Madison, Harriet Washington, and many of the connection staying for days, keeping up a prolonged merry-making.

The girls, vying with each other in obtaining mementos of the evening, cut in bits the Mechlin lace from Mr. Madison's shirt ruffles ; and amid a shower of rice, the laughing bride and groom drove off to Montpelier, his father's estate in Orange County, Virginia.

The close of the year, however, found them back in Philadelphia, where Mrs. Madison, laying aside the sober Quaker dress at her husband's desire, began for the first time to enjoy a little gay society, even going to Mrs. Washington's drawing-room, where she was warmly welcomed and congratulated.

Anna Payne, the little sister who had lived with Mrs. Madison from the time of her first marriage, grew up like a daughter of the house, and shared the responsibilities and pleasures until she married in 1804.

Some bright letters have come into my hands, written by one of their intimate friends, Sally McKean, the daughter of Governor McKean, and afterwards wife of

the Marquis d'Yrujo, the Minister from
Spain in 1796. She was handsome, gay,
and independent, and the following letters
give a graphic description of Philadelphia
society and fashions about that time.

TO ANNA PAYNE.

PHILADELPHIA, *June* 10, 1796.

MY DEAR ANNA, — Yours, dated the
19th of May, was handed to me the day before yesterday by one Mr. Grove, who . . .
And now, my dear Anna, we will have
done with judges and juries, courts, both
martial and partial, and we will speak a
little about Philadelphia and the fashions,
the beaux, Congress, and the weather. Do
I not make a fine jumble of them ? What
would Harper or beau Dawson say were
they to know it, ha, ha, — mind you laugh
here with me. Philadelphia never was
known to be so lively at this season as at
present ; for an accurate account of the
amusements, I refer you to my letter to
your sister Mary. I went yesterday to see
a doll, which has come from England,
dressed to show us the fashions, and I saw
besides a great quantity of millinery. Very

long trains are worn, and they are festooned
up with loops of bobbin, and small covered
buttons, the same as the dress: you are
not confined to any number of festoons,
but put them according to your fancy, and
you cannot conceive what a beautiful effect it has. There is also a robe which
is plaited very far back, open and ruffled
down the sides, without a train, being even
with the petticoat. The hats are quite a
different shape from what they used to be :
they have no slope in the crown, scarce
any rim, and are turned up at each side,
and worn very much on the side of the
head. Several of them are made of
chipped wood, commonly known as cane
hats; they are all lined : one that has come
for Mrs. Bingham is lined with white, and
trimmed with broad purple ribbon, put
round in large puffs, with a bow on the
left side. The bonnets are all open on
the top, through which the hair is passed,
either up or down as you fancy, but lat-
terly they wear it more up than down; it
is quite out of fashion to frizz or curl the
hair, as it is worn perfectly straight. Ear-
rings, too, are very fashionable. The
waists are worn two inches longer than

they used to be, and there is no such thing
as long sleeves. They are worn half way
above the elbow, either drawn or plaited in
various ways, according to fancy ; they do
not wear ruffles at all, and as for elbows,
Anna, ours would be alabaster, compared
to some of the ladies who follow the fashion ; black or a colored ribbon is pinned
round the bare arm, between the elbow
and the sleeve. There have come some
new-fashioned slippers for ladies, made of
various colored kid or morocco, with small
silver clasps sewed on ; they are very handsome, and make the feet look remarkably small and neat. Everybody thinks the
millinery last received the most tasty seen
for a long time.

All our beaux are well ; the amiable
Chevalier is perfectly recovered, and hand-
somer than ever. I mentioned to him last
evening that I had received a letter from
you, and that you desired to be remembered to him ; he seemed much pleased at
your attention, and desired that I should
give his best love to you when I wrote ;
so did Fatio and good Mr. Viar: so you
see, my dear Anna, I do keep my promise,
tho' you scold me so much. Mind that

you write me a long answer to this, and that very soon.

Your sincere and affectionate friend,
SALLY McKEAN.

TO ANNA PAYNE.

PHILADELPHIA, *September* 3, 1796.

MY DEAR ANNA, — I received yours by Mr. Taylor — and duly delivered its inclosure. You can have no idea, my dear girl, what pleasant times I have; there is the charming Chevalier, the divine Santana, the jolly Viar, the witty and agreeable Fatio, the black-eyed Lord Henry, the soft, love-making Count, the giggling, foolish ——, and sometimes the modest, good Meclare, who are at our house every day. We have fine riding-parties and musical frolics. However, I will refer you to my letter to your sister Madison, as I am tired of writing, this being my third letter to-day.

Mr. and Mrs. Jandenes set sail about the middle of July, with the two dear little children in good health and remarkably fine spirits. I am to have a large packet of papers from them as soon as they arrive in Spain, telling me all the news, and also a very elegant Spanish guitar, on

which I intend to learn to play. Signor
Don Carlos has given me a few lessons on
that instrument. I have one at present,
lent me by Santana, and we have a famous
Italian singer, who came with the Minister, who can play on any instrument, and
is moreover the drollest creature you ever
saw. He sings divinely, and is the leader
of our fine concerts. I am serenaded
every night with divine music. I must
say divine, for it is so much above the
common music.

I long with the greatest impatience for
the month of October, that I may have the
pleasure of embracing my dear Anna; for
Heaven's sake make as much haste to town
as you can, for we are to have one of the
most charming winters imaginable. Santana and Fatio send their compliments to
you, and Meclare told me to be sure to
give his best and most sincere love to you;
he looks quite handsome, and is smarter
than ever. God bless you, my dearest,
and believe me to be your sincere friend
and admirer,   SALLY McKEAN.

About this time Mr. Madison writes to
an old friend and schoolmate, Mr. Murray,

of Virginia, who was then Consul at Liverpool, which post he held for more than thirty years.

PHILADELPHIA, *January*, 18, 1797:

DEAR SIR, — Mr. Mason and myself lately received your packets of London papers by the " Alexander Hamilton," which were very acceptable, as they brought us the earliest accounts of some of the important articles contained in them. I send in return several packets by Captain Joseph Prince, who is to sail from New York, and to whom I cannot conveniently transmit anything of a more bulky nature. Captain Prince is a brother-in-law of Mr. Beckley, clerk of the House of Representatives, and formerly known to you in Virginia. He will be very sensible to any kindness it may be in your power to show his friend ; and they will have a proper claim on his acknowledgments also.

This country is extremely agitated by pecuniary distresses, and the mercantile troubles which begin to thicken. The unfortunate Treaty intended to appease the nation is bringing us into trouble with

several. You will see that the House of
Representatives is engaged on the question of a direct tax. The result is a prob-
lem not yet to be solved. It is expected
that the Executive will communicate in a
few days a full statement of the contro-
versy with France.

After a warm contest for the succession
to General Washington, the vacancy will
be filled by Mr. Adams. He has seventy-
one votes, and Mr. Jefferson only sixty-
eight. The division would be more, but
for the failure of one of the returns from
a county in this State in time to be counted, and other casualties in other States
had a share in favoring Mr. Adams. Mr.
Jefferson, it is now well known, will serve
in the secondary place allotted to him.

This being the last session of Congress
of which I shall be a member, I must, at
the same time that I return you thanks
for all your past favors, request that your
future ones be addressed to Orange County, Virginia, and that they may not be sent
on the calculation that I shall get them
free of postage.

With great esteem, I am, dear sir,
            Your obedient servant,
                  JAMES MADISON, JR.

CHAPTER IV.

In the year 1799, Mrs. Madison, accompanied by her husband, made her last visit to her uncle and aunt, Mr. and Mrs. Winston, who lived near her old home in Hanover County, Virginia. Colonel Isaac Winston was a man of cultivation and sound judgment, whom Mr. Madison regarded with the highest respect, and one of the few to whom he would yield his opinion. We find by letters received at different times much good advice given by this quiet country gentleman, — advice that was valued and acted upon.

A visit of condolence was also paid to Mrs. Washington at Mt. Vernon, by Mr. and Mrs. Madison, accompanied by Mr. Jefferson, after General Washington's death. Here it was that the intimacy began between Mrs. Madison and Miss Henley, a favorite niece and ward of Mrs. Washington, afterwards Mrs. Tobias Lear.

In 1801, Mr. Jefferson was elected President, Mr. Madison became Secretary of State, Albert Gallatin succeeded Mr. Dexter in the portfolio of the Treasury, and Mr. Dearborn was made Secretary of War. The other members of the Cabinet remained unchanged for a year or more. Happy and handsome, Mrs. Madison came on to Washington prepared to do her best with the duties and responsibilities before her. The position was in perfect accordance with her disposition. She was humble-minded, tolerant, and sincere, but with a desire to please, and a willingness to be pleased, which made her popular, and always a great friend and support to her husband. The power of adaptation was a life-giving principle in her nature, while an unusually retentive memory prevented her from ever forgetting either names, faces, or the slightest incident connected with the personal history of any one. Washington at that time was almost a wilderness. The houses were few and far between, while the streets, or rather roads, were at times almost impassable from mud. There was, however, a small and agreeable resident society in the three District cities, Alexandria, Washington, and Georgetown, where the entertainments began at seven o'clock and lasted until ten.

In those days, when steamboats were just beginning, railroads unknown, stage-coaches ingeniously uncomfortable, and even turnpike roads rare, journeys were made either on horseback, or in a private conveyance. The daughter of a Senator, who wished to enjoy the gayeties of the capital, accompanied her father five hundred miles on horseback. The wife of a member of Congress, being equally ambitious, rode fifteen hundred miles on horseback, passing through several Indian encampments on the way, and was for many nights without a house to lodge in. Mrs. Madison herself had traveled from her Virginia home by easy stages, incumbered with household furniture, occupying what seems to us in these days an incredible length of time.

Mr. Jefferson's two daughters being married and living in Virginia, Mrs. Madison, aided by her sister, usually presided at the White House, and was much depended upon, as a few of the many little notes received at various times will show : —

May 27, 1801.

Thomas Jefferson begs that either Mrs. Madison or Miss Payne will be so good as to dine with him to-day, to take care of female friends expected.

June 4, 1801.

Thomas Jefferson was much disappointed at breakfast this morning, not having until then known of the departure of Mr. and Mrs. Madison and Miss Payne ; he hopes they will come and dine to-day with the Miss Butters, who were assured they would meet them here, and to-morrow with Mrs. Gallatin and Mrs. Mason. Affectionate salutations.

July 10, 1805.

Thomas Jefferson presents his respectful thanks to Mrs. Madison for the trouble she has been so kind as to take on his behalf. Nothing more is wanting, unless (having forgotten little Virginia) a sash or something of that kind could be picked up anywhere for her. The amount, and the person from whom the earrings and pin were bought, Thomas Jefferson would also ask of Mrs. Madison. He presents his affectionate salutations.

Martha Jefferson, who married Mr. Randolph was able to pay two visits only to her father during his administration. She would have been particularly fitted to do the honors of the White House, having accompanied her father to Paris, when a child, where she was placed under the care of Madame de Genlis, and received a most thorough education, enjoying afterwards a glimpse of the brilliant French society just before the Revolution. She and Mrs. Madison became firm friends, and from being much together during her visits to Washington were sometimes taken for each other. On one occasion, having been induced to put on "a pelisse and hat to correspond" belonging to her friend, she made a number of visits to comparative strangers, announced invariably as Mrs. Madison.

Maria Jefferson, the youngest daughter, was very beautiful, but delicate; she married Mr. Eppes, of Virginia, and died while her father was President.

The following are the rules of etiquette formed and followed conscientiously by the President and his Cabinet:—

CANONS OF ETIQUETTE TO BE OBSERVED BY
THE EXECUTIVE.

By President Jefferson.

1st. Foreign Ministers arriving at the seat of government pay the first visit to the ministers of the nation, which is returned; and so likewise on subsequent occasions of reassembling after a recess.

2d. The families of foreign Ministers receive the first visit from those of the national Ministers, as from all other residents, and as all strangers, foreign or domestic, do from all residents of the place.

3d. After the first visit the character of stranger ceases.

4th. Among the members of the Diplomatic Corps, the Executive Government, in its own principles of personal and national equality, considers every Minister as the representative of his nation, and equal to every other without distinction of grade.

5th. No titles being admitted here, those of foreigners give no precedence.

6th. Our Ministers to foreign nations are as private citizens while here.

7th. At any public ceremony to which the Government invites the presence of foreign Ministers and their families, no precedence or privilege will be given them other than the provision of a convenient seat or station with any other stranger invited, and with the families of the National Ministers.

8th. At dinners, in public or private, and on all other occasions of social intercourse, a perfect equality exists between the persons composing the company, whether foreign or domestic, titled or untitled, in or out of office.

9th. To give force to the principle of equality, or *pêle mêle*, and prevent the growth of precedence out of courtesy, the members of the Executive, at their own houses, will adhere to the ancient usage of their ancestors, — gentlemen *en masse* giving place to the ladies *en masse*.

10th. The President of the United States receives visits, but does not return them.

11th. The family of the President receives the first visit and returns it.

12th. The President and his family take precedence everywhere, in public, or private.

13th. The President when in any State receives the first visit from the Governor and returns it.

14th. The Governor in his State receives the first visit from a foreign Minister.

The next two or three years passed
smoothly and pleasantly to Mr. and Mrs.
Madison; he, absorbed in his work, and
always a great reader, left all social duties
to her, and we get glimpses of their many
entertainments through her letters.

When the first Turkish Minister, Méléy
Méléy, arrived in Washington a grand ball
was given in his honor, to which the beauty
and fashion of the town flocked, curious to
see his elaborate dress, and turban made
of plaster of Paris, representing the finest
muslin   He, however, showed perfect indifference to the open admiration about
him, until spying a large, fat negress on
her way from the kitchen, he rushed to
her, and with much enthusiasm threw his
arms around her, saying she reminded him
of home and his best and most expensive
wife, " A load for a camel."

TO MRS. GENERAL MASON.

I am obliged, my charming friend, to
announce to you the disappointment in my

hopes of attending your agreeable party to Alexandria, as some imperative domestic engagements forbid (to me) such an indulgence, — I know you will be good enough to make my apology to Madame Buonaparte, and if my sister can contribute to your pleasant excursion, she will go with great cheerfulness.

With affectionate salutations to the ladies of your house, believe me,

Truly yours,   D. P. MADISON.

In February, 1803, Captain Lewis and Captain Clark were sent by Mr. Jefferson to explore the Missouri River, and discover the best communication with the Pacific Ocean. The ladies of the Cabinet, particularly Mrs. Madison, were most interested and sympathetic, providing everything that could possibly be needed in such a perilous journey, fearing they might never return from the distant land of savages.

Mr. Jefferson writes to his friend, Dr. Barton, of Philadelphia, of this interesting expedition : —

It was impossible to find a man who, to a complete science in Botany, Natural

History, Mineralogy, and Astronomy, joined the firmness of constitution and character, prudence, habits adapted to the woods, and familiarity with the Indian manners and habits requisite for this undertaking.

All the latter qualifications Lewis has; although no real botanist, etc., he possesses a remarkable store of accurate information on all subjects of the three kingdoms, and will therefore readily single out whatever presents itself new to him in either, and he has qualified himself for taking the longitude and latitude necessary to fix the geography of the line he passes through. In order to draw his attention at once to the objects most desirable, I must ask of you to prepare for him a note of those in the lines of Botany, Zoölogy, or of Indian history which you think most worthy of observation.

Sincerely your friend,
Thomas Jefferson.

In the same year Gilbert Stuart, the celebrated portrait painter, came to Washington, and was very cordially received. It became the fashion to have a " Stuart por·

trait," and his time was soon very fully taken up. A friend writes to Mrs. Madison, who was away temporarily : " I can tell you nothing new. Stuart is all the rage, he is almost worked to death, and every one afraid that they will be the last to be finished." He says, " The ladies come and say, *dear* Mr. Stuart I am afraid you will be very much tired ; you really must rest when my picture is done."

His great success seemed to lie in his power to interest and amuse the sitters so that they forgot themselves, and appeared simply and naturally. Both Mr. and Mrs. Madison were painted with very favorable results.

CHAPTER V.

In 1804, Mrs. Madison writes : " One of the greatest griefs of my life has come to me, in the parting for the first time from my sister-child."

This favorite sister, the little Anna, who had been her constant companion always, married Richard Cutts, a member of Congress from the District of Maine, then constituting a part of the Commonwealth of Massachusetts. A clever, well-educated man, having studied both at Harvard University and in Europe, he was chosen to represent his district at the age of twenty-eight, and remained through six successive Congresses. He was taken immediately into the warm heart of his sister-in-law, and the wedding was a scene of great gayety, forming an irresistible opportunity for Mrs. Madison to give pleasure to everybody. The wedding-presents of eighty years ago differed from the present gorgeous display of jewels, bric-a-brac, etc., inasmuch as they were tokens of love or friendship made by the hand of the friend, elaborate embroideries from sleeves to pincushions, paintings and original poetry ; the wife of the Russian Minister, Madame Dashcoff, sent the usual wedding present of her country — two wine-coolers, one filled with salt, the essence of life, and the other with bread, the staff of life. Parson McCormick performed the ceremony. He had charge of the only church in Washington at that time, a church at the Navy Yard, to which the President and Cabinet were obliged to drive two or three miles through muddy roads to attend service. To avoid this he very often preached in the Hall of the State or Treasury Department.

TO ANNA CUTTS.

April 26, 1804.

Though few are the days passed since you left me, my dearest Anna, they have been spent in anxious impatience to hear from you. Your letter from Baltimore relieved my mind, and the one from Philadelphia this hour received gives me the greatest pleasure. To trace you and your

dear husband in that regretted city, where
we have spent our early years, to find that
even there you can recollect with affection
the solitary being you have left behind, re-
flects a ray of brightness on my sombre
prospects. I will now give you a little
sketch of our times here. I shut myself
up from the time you entered the stage
until Saturday, when we went to drive in
the rain with Marshall Brent. All our acquaintance called in to see me on the different mornings. Those few whom I saw
seemed to sympathize with me in your
loss !!! I drank tea with the Fingeys and
Mrs. Forest, the amount of visits accom-
plished. A letter from the President announces the death of poor Maria, and the
consequent misery it has occasioned them
all. This is among the many proofs, my
dear sister, of the uncertainty of life. A
girl so young, so lovely! All the efforts
of friends and doctors availed nothing. I
am delighted with the kind attention you
meet from our old acquaintance, and have
no doubt but that you will have a grateful
welcome in all the places you are destined
to visit. Remember me to the McKeans,
and to Sally say a great deal, for I feel a

tenderness for her and her husband, independent of circumstances.

Your devoted sister, DOLLY.

TO MRS. MADISON FROM HER SISTER.

BOSTON, *May*, 1804.

MY DEAREST DOLLY, — How I miss you it would not be possible to say. The town of Boston is all confusion, no regularity anywhere, and after Philadelphia and New York it seemed as if I should be stifled; the situations and prospects outside of the town are delightful, but you have heard from others, more capable of describing it. We have very pleasant lodgings, and for my companion the famous Madame Knox, who although very haughty I find pleasant and sensible. Chess is now her mania, which she plays extremely well, only too often for my fancy, who am not of late so partial to it. Every morning after breakfast, there is a summons from her ladyship, which if I attend pins me to her apron-string until time to dress for dinner, after which she retires, again inviting me to battle. Out of twenty-one games, in only two, and a drawn game, has she shown me any mercy; she is certainly

the most successful player I ever encoun-
tered. Thursday we dined at the Mortons',
an extremely pleasant place, the house
and grounds quite tasteful. Mrs. Morton
strikes one most at home, believe me, and
had I her establishment would n'ever quit
it for anything in Washington. She has
four fine daughters, all women, and two of
them very pretty. They gave us a handsome dinner and a pleasant party, with a
dash at Loo in the evening, to please Mrs.
Knox, I suppose. The Federal party in
Boston prevails, — however, in spite of my
connections, I find much civility among
them. Always, my dearly beloved sister,
much love, in which my husband joins me.

Yours devotedly,   ANNA.

This Mrs. Knox who was so fond of
chess was the wife of Washington's favorite general, and the owner of one of the
handsomest places in Maine, at Thomas-
ton ; of which Mrs. Madison's sister writes
to her : " We have not yet made our visit
to General Knox, though we have received
many pressing invitations to hasten to do
so. It is more than an hundred miles from
us, and I have an antipathy to make such

an addition to my journey, notwithstanding my desire to see the country, and most
of all their princely establishment, which
is the wonder of the eastern world."

Mrs. Knox's mother was engaged at one
time to the son of Sir William Pepperell,
and great preparations were made for the
wedding. A house was built and furnished
— everything was done that money and
love could do to smooth the way of the
happy young couple. At the wedding,
however, standing before the clergyman, in
the midst of a gay party of friends, the
bride suddenly changed her mind and
walked up stairs, saying she had decided
not to marry. Two days after this the
bridegroom dropped dead in the street.

TO ANNA.

WASHINGTON, *June*, 1804.

MY DEAREST ANNA, — How delighted
I should be to accompany you to all the
charming places you mentioned, to see all
the kind people, and to play Loo with Mrs.
Knox. Mr. Madison would write, but is
overwhelmed with business. The British,
French, and Spanish infringements are all
under his pen ; he expects General A.

every day, who is to succeed Mr. Livingstone, to receive his instructions. He always sends his affectionate love. Mount
Vernon has been set on fire five different
times, and it is suspected some malicious
persons are determined to reduce it to
ashes. Oh, the wickedness of men and
women! I am afraid to accept their invitations.

WASHINGTON, *July* 16, 1804.

MY DEAREST ANNA,—Yours from Maine
reached me yesterday, and I need not say
how delighted I am at your description of
places and persons, and at the knowledge
of your felicity. We go to Montpelier
this week. Payne continues weak and
sick ; and my prospects rise and fall to
sadness as this precious child recovers or
declines. You have heard, no doubt, of
the terrible duel and death of poor Hamilton. I sent the President word of your
offer to get the glass, etc.

TO MRS. ISAAC WINSTON.

April 9, 1804.

I consider myself a most unlucky being,
my dearest aunt, in regard to my letters
to you, for you certainly cannot have received my two last or you would have al-
luded to them in yours, which we have
this moment received. What must my
dear uncle think of me! but I will now
take the opportunity to scold you for not
knowing my heart better, which has always been open to you, — you speak to me
in apologies for my Cousin Dolly's stay,
when I have considered it as a favor, and a
very great pleasure, only wishing we could
live together all our lives. We hope and
expect to go to you in May. Public business, perhaps, was never thicker. I have
just received a long letter from mamma,
who is quite well, and I pray that your
fears may not be realized, my dear aunt,
but that you may yet spend a great deal
of time together in this life. I should be
miserable, indeed, if I did not feel such a
conviction. I am taking care of my best
prunes and figs for you. Tell dear uncle
I am ashamed to speak to him, but he will

see by this that it was not my fault. Farewell, dearest aunt, I have nothing new to tell you as you must know all about Burr.

   Ever your devoted,   DOLLY.

Missing the companionship of her sister and craving sympathy and love always, Mrs. Madison persuaded her Cousin, Dolly Winston, to live with her for a time, and later on Anna Payne, her brother's child, took her place, and became like a daughter in her old age, remaining with her until her death. In the years when the kind, unselfish old lady found herself too weak to wield a pen, she begged her niece to copy her handwriting, not to disappoint the many who valued little notes from her, which she did so successfully that the harmless subterfuge was never discovered.

In the spring of 1804 Baron Humboldt came to Washington, and Mrs. Madison writes of his attractiveness to the absent sister, whom she kept informed of everything she was doing and thinking: —

We spent last evening at Mr. Pichon's.
Our city is now almost deserted, and will
be more so in a week or two. Dr. and
Mrs. T. sat yesterday for the last time to
Stuart. He has now nearly finished all his
portraits, and says he means to go directly
to Boston, but that is what he has said
these two years; being a man of genius,
he of course does things differently from
other people. I hope he will be here next
winter, as he has bought a square to build
a "Temple" upon. Where will you cele-
brate the Fourth of July, my dear sister?
We are to have grand doings here. Mr.
Van Ness is to deliver an oration, Mr. L.
says, in the woods, and the ladies are to
be permitted to partake of the mirth. We
have lately had a great treat in the company of a charming Prussian Baron. All
the ladies say they are in love with him,
notwithstanding his want of personal
charms. He is the most polite, modest,
well-informed, and interesting traveller we
have ever met, and is much pleased with
America. I hope one day you will become
acquainted with our charming Baron Hum-

boldt.   He sails in a few days for France
with his companions, and is going to pub-
lish an account of his travels in South
America, where he lived five years ; proposing to return here again.   He had with
him a train of philosophers, who, though
clever and entertaining, did not compare
to the Baron.

TO ANNA.

May 22, 1804.

I am always rejoiced to hear from you,
dearest Anna, and glad you have recovered
my letters.   There is so much I could tell
you about these new French people, things
that could not fail to divert you, but I
must forbear, and am learning to hold my
tongue well.   Madame —— shows me
everything she has, and would fain give
me of everything.   She decorates herself
according to the French ideas, and urges
me to do the same.   She is very anxious
to see my " belle sœur," as she styles you,
and oh ! Anna, I'm dying to come to your
country ; if I could only be with you how
glad I should be.

TO ANNA.

MONTPELIER, *June* 3, 1804.

I have received all your letters, my dear-est Anna, one from Boston, in which my dear brother adds his mite of amusement for Madison and myself, with one from your own house. I rejoice more in the last ; the former frightened me a little, but we hope from the public prints that we shall not be quite outdone by the Feder-alists this time. We are still in Orange, and shall not leave it before the 9th or 10th. I have been very ill since I wrote last, with inflammatory rheumatism ; never had I more extreme pain in sickness. Dr. Willis bled me, and Mother Madison nursed, and waited upon me with great at-tention and kindness. We have had a continual round of company, which has been burdensome, though I 've had no trouble with it ; the day I was most ill, fifteen or twenty of the family and connec-tion dined here, and I did not quit my bed, or know anything about them. I have a long letter from the Marchioness d'Yrujo, who speaks of you like a good friend. Ah! my dear, you little know the triumph

I feel when I hear of you and your beloved husband in the way that so many speak of you! If Payne was a man, married, and gone from me, I could not feel more sensibly everything that regarded him than I do for you both. Stuart has taken an admirable likeness of Mr. Madison ; both his and mine are finished.

Devotedly yours,

DOLLY P. MADISON.

CHAPTER VI.

ALWAYS amiable and conciliatory in dealing with friends or slaves, Mrs. Madison's popularity grew day by day. Her politeness was that which comes from the heart, and cannot be imitated by those who have not the love and sympathy ready to be called forth at all times.

She complains of being "put forward by Mr. Jefferson," to her sister Anna (who spent a part of every year in Maine), and describes a state dinner at the "White House" to which many of the Diplomats were invited, when, to her surprise, the President stepped forward and offered her his arm, as the wife of the Secretary of State; she demurred, and whispered, "Take Mrs. Merry" (the wife of the British Minister); but firmly refusing, she was obliged then and always, during his administration, to take the head of the table. Mrs. Merry, feeling deeply insulted, seized her husband's arm, and walked in behind them;

afterwards they complained to their government of bad treatment, and were recalled.

She used to tell a little anecdote of herself, at the time when delegations of Indians were brought to Washington on one plea or another, and entertained by the Cabinet. After a supper given to some of these red men by the Secretary of State, Mrs. Madison, on the point of retiring, happened to look in her mirror, and saw there the reflection of an Indian in all his war paint, behind the door ; taking care not to catch his eye, she paused a moment to avoid suspicion, then walking quietly into the other room, rang the bell, and returned to her toilet. The bell was answered by a tall negro, who, with her help, gently persuaded the astonished man that he had made a mistake.

In 1805 Mrs. Madison injured her knee, which, on being neglected, threatened to prove a serious accident, and she writes despondingly of recovery.

WASHINGTON, *June* 4, 1805.

MY DEAREST ANNA, — I write to you from my bed, to which I have been con-

fined for ten days with a bad knee; it has
become very painful, and two doctors have
applied caustic with the hope of getting
me well, but Heaven only knows! I feel
as if I should never walk again. My dear
husband insists upon taking me to Philadelphia to be under Dr. Physic's care, but
he cannot stay with me, and I dread the
separation.

Yesterday we had brother George,
Thornton, and Lawrence Washington to
spend the day, and I enjoyed the sound
of Virginia hilarity echoing through the
house; George coughs incessantly, looks
thin and hoarse, but has no idea of dying.
Since I wrote you two days past, I have
heard sad things of Tourreau, — that he
whips his wife, and abuses her dreadfully;
I pity her sincerely; she is an amiable,
sensible woman. A letter from Mount
Vernon begging me to come there, but
alas! I shall walk no more.

Yours ever, DOLLY.

General Tourreau was Minister from
France under the reign of Égalité, and his
career seems to have been one character-
istic of that period. Of obscure birth, but

handsome and clever, he made his way up, and became an aide to Napoleon Bonaparte.

In the rapid changes of popular favor, he, who had shown nothing but extreme cruelty when in power, was condemned to death, and his door marked with the fatal guide to the bloody guillotiners. A servant-girl employed about the jail, taking a rude interest in the handsome gentleman, rubbed out the mark and so saved his life, in return for which he married her; the alliance, of course, proved to be a most unhappy one, ending in a separation at the time he was representing his country in Washington.

TO ANNA.

WASHINGTON, *July* 8, 1805.

Still, my dear Anna, must your sister write to you from the bed. My knee will keep me in Washington longer, I fear, than will be conducive to our health or interest. I have nothing new to tell you, for the town is dull and vacant. The President goes in a week, and we were all to go about the same time, but for the reason given. I feel now very impatient to be in Montpelier, and have confidence in

the change of air, though this place seems
to be healthy, if terribly warm and dry.
I had a long friendly note from the President yesterday, begging me to get Virginia's (his granddaughter) wedding gar-
ments, also trinkets and dresses for all the
family. I shall drive to the shops, but am
not able to alight; and so little variety in
Georgetown; but I must do my best for
them, and have promised to be at the wedding, if possible, the last of this month.
But I have scarcely a wish, and no expec-
tation of going. How I should rejoice to
be with you, dear Anna, though I could
not have the pleasure of playing nurse to
you now, as I never leave my room but to
drive. The Fourth of July I spent at the
President's, sitting quite still, and amusing
myself with the mob. Farewell.

Your own sister, DOLLY.

TO ANNA.

PHILADELPHIA, *July* 29, 1805.

If my beloved sister has received my
last from Washington, she will be unhappy
to find that I was obliged to take this journey in such dangerously hot weather, but
it proved not unpleasant, for I was easier

riding than in any other position. My
health and spirits revived every day with
the drive, and here I am on my bed, with
my dear husband sitting anxiously by me,
who is my most willing nurse. But you
know how delicate he is. I tremble for
him ; one night on the way he was taken
very ill with his old complaint, and I could
not fly to aid him as I used to do. Heaven
in its mercy restored him next morning,
and he would not pause until he heard my
fate from Doctor Physic.

Your devoted sister,   DOLLY.

TO ANNA.

PHILADELPHIA, *July* 31, 1805.

MY DEAR SISTER, — We are in excellent lodgings on Sansom Street, and I feel
like another being. Dr. Physic has put
my knee in splints and promises me a
cure in time. I have the world to see me,
and many invitations to the houses of the
gentry, but withstand all, to be at ease
here. I have not seen where I am, yet,
and the longer I stay, the less do the vanities tempt me, though, as you know, I
usually like the routs all too well. You
ask who is kindest to me here, and I can

tell you that, among a number, Betsey
Pemberton bears off the palm. Never
can I forget Betsey, who has been to me
what you would have been. I have had a
lecture from S. L. on seeing too much
company, and it brought to my mind the
time when our society used to control me
entirely, and debar me from so many advantages and pleasures ; even now, I feel
my ancient terror revive in a great degree.
Madison is well, though besieged with callers ; he sends his love to you both, as I do.

Ever your devoted   DOLLY.

Dr. Physic, an eminent physician in
Philadelphia, having promised to cure the
lame knee, Mr. Madison, with great reluctance, left her and returned to Washington, to his official duties ; from there he
writes frequently of his loneliness and anxiety. This, almost the first separation
since their marriage, seems to have been
great pain, too, to Mrs. Madison, and she
writes full of anxiety for his health, after
the long weary drive from Philadelphia to
Washington, albeit he was put under the
care of their faithful attendant, " black
Peter."

TO MR. MADISON.

PHILADELPHIA, *October* 23, 1805.

A few hours only have passed since you left me, my beloved, and I find nothing can relieve the oppression of my mind but speaking to you, in this, the only way. Dr. Physic called before you had gone far, but I could only find voice to tell him my knee felt better. Betsey Pemberton and Amy (her maid) are sitting by me, and seem to respect the grief they know I feel at even so short a separation from one who is all to me. I shall be better when Peter returns with news, not that any length of time could lessen my first regret, but an assurance that you are well and easy will contribute to make me so. I have sent the books and note to Mrs. D. Betsey puts on your hat to divert me, but I cannot look at her.

October 24. — What a sad day! The watchman announced a cloudy morning at one o'clock, and from that moment I found myself unable to sleep, from anxiety for thee, my dearest husband. Detention, cold, and accident seem to menace thee. Betsey, who lay beside me, admin-

istered several drops of laudanum, which
had a partial effect. Every one is most
kind and attentive.

October 25. — This clear, cold morning
will favor your journey, and enliven the
feelings of my darling. I have nothing
new to tell you. The knee is mending,
and I sit just as you left me. The doctor,
during his short visits, talks of you. He
regards you more than any man he knows,
and nothing could please him so much as
a prospect of passing his life near you ;
sentiments so congenial to my own, and in
such cases, like dew-drops on flowers, ex-
hilarate as they fall. The Governor, I
hear, has arrived, and is elated with his
good fortune. General Moreau is expected
in town very shortly, to partake of a grand
dinner the citizens are about to give him.
Adieu, my beloved, our hearts understand
each other. In fond affection thine,

DOLLY P. MADISON.

TO MR. MADISON.

PHILADELPHIA, *October* 26, 1805.

MY DEAREST HUSBAND, — Peter returned safe with your dear letter, and
cheered me with a favorable account of

the prospects of your getting home in the stage. I was sorry you could not ride further in our carriage, as it might have spared you fatigue.

In my dreams of last night, I saw you in your chamber, unable to move, from riding so far and so fast. I pray that an early letter from you may chase away the painful impression of this vision. I am still improving, and shall observe strictly what you say on the subject of the doctor's precepts.

October 28. — I have this moment received the letters you inclosed from Washington. I rejoice to hear you are there, and shall await the next post with impatience ; by that, you will speak of yourself. The Marquis and Marchioness came to see me yesterday, with many other friends. I am getting well as fast as I can, for I have the reward in view of then seeing my beloved. Tell me if Mrs. Randolph is expected, and all the news you shall have time and patience to give me. I have written you every day since we parted, but am so shut up that I can say nothing to amuse ; when I begin to drive out, I hope to become a more interesting

correspondent. Did you see the Bishop,
or engage a place at school for Payne?
Farewell, until to-morrow, my best friend;
think of thy wife, who thinks and dreams
of thee.   DOLLY.

TO MR. MADISON.

PHILADELPHIA, *October* 30, 1805.

I have at this moment perused with delight thy letter, my darling husband, with
its inclosures. To find you love me, have
my child safe, and that my mother is well,
seems to comprise all my happiness. The
doctor has ordered me some drops, which
I take dutifully. I walk about the room,
and hope a few days more will enable me
to ride, so that you may expect me to fly
to you as soon — ah! I wish I might say
how soon. Madame Pichon writes me an
affectionate letter, and begs me to accept
a pair of ear-rings for her sake. You no
doubt have them, as they are not with the
letter. I am punctual in delivering to
Betsey all your commands, and she insists
on adding a postscript to this which I am
not to see. I have also a letter from the
President, asking me to procure several
articles for Mrs. Randolph, which I shall

soon be able to do, by driving to the shop doors. There have been many callers to-day, and pressing invitations. It is now past nine o'clock, and I cease to write, only to dream of thee. Tell Mrs. Thornton I am having the model of a bonnet made for her; the new ones are just coming in. Write soon to thy devoted

DOLLY.

TO MR. MADISON.

PHILADELPHIA, *November* 1, 1805.

I have great pleasure, my beloved, in repeating to you what the doctor has just told me — that I may reasonably hope to leave this place in a fortnight; I am so impatient to be restored to you. I wish you would indulge me with some information respecting the war with Spain, and the disagreement with England, which is so generally expected. You know I am not much of a politician, but I am extremely anxious to hear (as far as you think proper) what is going forward in the Cabinet. On this subject, I believe you would not desire your wife to be the active partisan that our neighbor is, Mrs. L., nor will there be the slightest danger, while she is conscious of her want of talents, and the diffidence in expressing those opinions, always imperfectly understood by her sex. Kiss my child for me, and remember me to my friends. Adieu, my dear husband. Peter brings me no letter from you, which really unfits me from writing more to any one.

Your ever affectionate   DOLLY.

TO MR. MADISON.

PHILADELPHIA, *November* 15, 1805.

MY DARLING HUSBAND, — I have just parted from Colonel Patton, who is well pleased with the payment of the horses, and congratulated me on possessing such a handsome pair. I went to pay some visits this morning, and on my return found Anthony Morris waiting, with a petition from his wife that I would let him wait upon me to her house for some days; but am too fearful of taxing my strength, much as I love these old and dear friends. I see that Jackson's paper has announced the declaration of war from Spain against us, and that the Marquis d'Yrujo has requested his passport. He was here with other company last evening. Mrs. Stewart inquired if this was true, and he became terribly angry. Thureau is ill, but goes abroad too. The impression of him in Philadelphia is a sad one; he is remembered as the cruel commander at La Vendée, and the fighting husband. I am about to put up the articles for the President, and will inclose a note for you, too.

November 17. — Anna and her husband arrived last evening, my beloved, and so pleased and agitated was I, that I could not sleep. We will leave on Monday, if I am quite strong enough; but I will wait your commands. Farewell, my beloved one.   DOLLY.

Having entirely recovered from all trouble with her knee, Mrs. Madison, to her great joy, joined her husband and child in Washington. From there they went for a month or two in summer to the dearly-loved Montpelier, and she writes in great grief, at hearing of the death of a little niece and namesake.

TO MRS. JOHN PAYNE.

MONTPELIER, *August* 4, 1806.

Expressions are wanting, my dearest mother, to convey to you my feelings ; I have not been very well since hearing from poor Mary, and it seems to me I can never feel as I have done. Dolly and Lucy both gone! they are now angels, and can never know evil or misery ; ought we not to console ourselves with this reflection ? I trust my beloved mother, whose trials have been so many, will exercise her fortitude, which is to preserve her for those of us that are left. I wrote thee by the last post, and have written repeatedly to John, but received only the inclosed letters. I shall now look out for vessels going to the Mediterranean, and write by them to him ; thine for him, thee had better inclose to me. Payne is to follow us in the stage on the 14th ; I am looking for a letter to cheer me with news of thy health.　　Ever thine, affectionately,

DOLLY.

TO ANNA.

WASHINGTON, *March* 27, 1807.

I am grieved, my dear Anna, at not hearing a word from you since you left us! What can be the matter? If the precious children engross your time, surely my good brother would think to relieve my anxiety by writing himself. This is the twelfth day of your absence, and I know not where to direct to you, but shall venture this to Philadelphia; the postmaster will forward it, should you be gone. Mr. Madison is very unwell with a cold, but is able to go to the office. We see no certain prospect of going to Orange yet. The President has a sick headache every day, and is obliged to retire to a dark room every morning by nine o'clock; he will not leave this until April 6th. I suppose you have heard that Burr is retaken, and on his way to Richmond for trial. We are quiet, and have but few parties. We went to the wedding feast of Miss Stoddard, and dined last Saturday with Mr. Erskine. Miss Clinton is still here with her father, but they have sent for a vessel, and intend sailing in a few days.

Ever thy loving sister,   DOLLY.

Always taking an intense interest in every movement of this favorite sister, whose children were, as she says, like her own grandchildren, Mrs. Madison kept up a constant correspondence through the long summers of those eight years when, with one sister in Maine and one in Virginia, the "post" must indeed have been anxiously watched for. What might not happen during the days and weeks that it took a letter to travel from one to the other?

TO ANNA.

MONTPELIER, *August* 28, 1808.

With heartfelt joy, my beloved sister, did I receive the short letter of my brother, giving the good tidings of your third son, and the promising health of you both. Mr. Madison, Lucy, George, and Payne were with me, and we all clapped our hands in triumph. The post did not come for a week after the letter, or I should have written you directly; and since that we have passed nearly a week at Monticello. Mrs. Randolph has a third son likewise, and she calls him Benjamin Franklin. Ann is to be married on the 15th, and I left them busy in their preparations. The Monroes were at their seat near here, but I did not see much of them.

Lucy left me on the 24th, and George seemed no better. We expect to go back to the city the last of September, because of public business. The President and Madison have been greatly perplexed by the remonstrances from so many towns to remove the Embargo. You see they refer to Congress, and the evading it is a terrible thing. Madison is uneasy and feels bound to return to the seat of government, where I shall be sorry to go so soon. The hope of my meeting you, dear Anna, is the chief sweetener to my prospect. The family here are as they always are, most affectionate and kind, and send a thousand loves to you. I expect a large party to fill the house next week.

Ever thy   DOLLY.

TO MRS. MADISON.

WASHINGTON, *August* 17, 1809.

MY DEAREST, —We reached the end of our journey yesterday at one o'clock, without interruption of any sort on the road. Mr. Coles had been here some time, and

one, if not two, of the expected despatch
vessels of England had just arrived, and
Mr. Gilston, after a short passage from
France, entered Washington about the moment I did. You may guess, therefore, the
volumes of papers before us. I am but
just dipping into them, and have seen no
one as yet, except Mrs. Smith for a few
minutes last evening. What number of
days I may be detained here it is impossible to say. The period, you may be sure,
will be shortened as much as possible.
Everything around and within reminds me
that you are absent, and makes me anxious
to quit this solitude. I hope in my next
to be able to say when I may have this
gratification, perhaps also to say something
of the intelligence just brought us. I send
the paper of this morning, which has something on the subject, and I hope the com-
munications of Gilston will be found more
favorable than is stated. Those from England can scarcely be favorable when such
men hold the reins. Mr. and Mrs. Erskine
are here. His successor had not sailed on
the 20th of June.

God bless you, and be assured of my
constant affection.   JAMES MADISON.

CHAPTER VII.

JEFFERSON'S administration was now drawing to a close. The territorial area of the United States had been greatly extended. Burr's wicked and dangerous conspiracy had come to naught. Pioneers were pouring into the Valley of the Mississippi. Explorers had crossed the mountains of the great West. The woods by the river-shores resounded with the blow of the axe. But the foreign relations of the United States were troubled and gloomy, and there were serious forebodings of war. The President, following the example of Washington, declined a third election, and was succeeded by James Madison, with George Clinton for Vice-President, in 1809. Mr. Madison owed his election to the Democratic party, whose sympathy with France and hostility to Great Britain were well known. Three days before the new administration came into power, the Embargo Act was repealed by Congress; but another measure was adopted instead, called the Non - Intercourse Act. By its terms American merchantmen were allowed to go abroad, but were forbidden to trade with Great Britain.

The affairs of the two nations were fast approaching a crisis. It became more and more evident that the wrongs perpetrated by England against the United States would have to be corrected by force of arms. The ministry of that same George III., with whom the Colonies had struggled in the Revolution, still directed the affairs of the kingdom; from him, now grown old and insane, nothing was to be expected. The elections held between 1808 and 1811 showed conclusively the drift of public opinion; the sentiment of the country was that war was preferable to further humiliation and disgrace. In 1809, Mr. Jefferson writes: "The belligerent edicts rendered our Embargo necessary to call home our ships, our seamen and property. We expected some effect, too, from the coercion of interest. Some, it *has* had, but much less on account of evasions and domestic opposition to it. After fifteen months' continuance it is now stopped, be-

cause by losing so much money annually
it really costs more than war. War therefore must follow unless the edicts are repealed before the meeting of Congress."

Many and sincere were the congratulations received by Mrs. Madison on going
into the White House. Every one in
Washington felt that her watchful care
and friendly interest would in no wise be
diminished by her advancement to a higher
position; and the magical effect of her
dainty snuff-box was as potent in one capacity as another. Political feuds ran high,
and party spirit was never more virulent
than at that time. The elements were
various and difficult to harmonize; yet she
was loved by all parties, and embittered
politicians, who never met save at her hospitable board, forgot all their quarrels under the influence of her gracious tact.
During the eight years of her life as wife
of the Secretary of State, she dispensed
with a liberal hand the abundant wealth
she prized so little, and the poor of the
District loved her name as that of a household deity. Finding time always among
her many social and domestic duties to
take her part in the administration of the

local charities, I find her name down in the
books of the Washington Orphan Asylum
(now one of the most prosperous in the
country), as one of the first directresses,
and the donor of twenty dollars and a
cow. The forms and ceremonials which
rendered Mrs. Washington's and Mrs.
Adams's drawing-rooms dull and tiresome
were laid aside, and no stiffness of any
kind was permitted. She returned all calls
made her by her own sex, and the " dove
parties," composed of the wives of Cabinet Officers and foreign Ministers, when
their lords were engaged in formal dinners, were exceedingly popular and lively.
Her private parties, and the lotteries in
which every guest received a " Cadeau,"
are still remembered with great pleasure
by a few. Though in no sense a learned
woman, nor one who at any time cared for
study, or even for reading, Dolly Madison
was eminently a talented woman, full of a
most delicate tact, and so warm-hearted
and amiable that even her early Quaker
friends were induced to condone what
they feared was " an undue fondness for
the things of this world." Thirty-seven
years of age, still very young in appear-

ance and feelings, she dressed handsomely
and "in the mode," clinging for a time to
the pretty little Quaker cap, but discarding
that even, when she went into the White
House, as unsuitable to her surroundings.
She was ambitious in that she endeavored
to make her husband's administration a
brilliant and successful one. With all her
appreciation of admiration she was not
extravagant, though hospitable to a degree which was rarely seen out of Virginia. She delighted in company, and her
table fairly "groaned," as the saying is,
with the abundance of its dishes. The
serious, thoughtful Madison, physically
weak, and harassed and worried by the
many cares crowding upon him at this
time, often said that a visit to his wife in
her sitting-room, where he was sure of a
bright story and a good laugh, was as re-
freshing as a long walk. And it was for
this end, to cheer and amuse her husband,
that she kept a pleasant party of friends
constantly with her, making them feel that
her home was theirs in the warmth of her
hospitality. An early riser, she superin-
tended all the domestic arrangements before breakfast, and while her guests were

still sleeping. The servants, many of whom were slaves, identified themselves entirely with the family, vying with each other in waiting on "Miss Dolly;" and at Montpelier, wherever the click of her high-heeled shoes was to be heard, a train of small negroes was sure to be seen waiting for the "sweety," accompanied by a bright smile, which never failed them.

TO ANNA.

WASHINGTON, *December* 20, 1811.

MY DEAREST ANNA, — I received with joy your letter last evening, which, being longer than usual, raised my spirits, which have been rather low in these troublous times. No Constitution heard of yet; the Hornet went to take despatches and to let them know our determination to fight for our rights. I wrote by the Hornet to Mrs. Barlow, and begged her to send me anything she thought suitable in the way of millinery. I fear I cannot obtain a new-fashioned pattern for you, but will make you a cap such as is much worn. The intrigues for President and Vice-President go on, but I think it may terminate as the last did. The Clintons, Smiths, Arm-

strongs, et cetera, are all in the field, and I
believe there will be war. Mr. Madison
sees no end to the perplexities without it,
and they seem to be going on with the
preparations. General Dearborn, you know,
is nominated to command. Congress talks
of adjourning for two months, but I believe it is merely a threatening, and they
will sit until June.   Before then I trust
you will be able to come on, as the roads
become passable by April.

> Devotedly your sister,
>   DOLLY MADISON.

A few extracts from the letters passing
between Mrs. Madison and her sister during the next year, when matters were approaching a crisis between the United
States and Great Britain, give a little insight into her thought and feelings.   Mr.
Madison too kept up a most regular correspondence with his brother-in-law, who
was obliged to spend that winter in Maine,
owing to an accident to his shoulder, ren-
dering the interminable carriage drive to
Washington impossible.

TO HON. RICHARD CUTTS.

WASHINGTON, *February* 25, 1812.

MY DEAR CUTTS, — I inclose for your amusement a few papers of the latest date. You will see that the Constitution has returned from France, and that an arrival from Great Britain has brought the speech opening the British Parliament. The latter decides nothing as to a change of the Cabinet, or repeal of the Orders in Council. Its tone on the whole is not arrogant. It is silent as to Russia and to Ireland, and as to trade and revenue. Distress may possibly supply motives, which ought to be found in wisdom and justice, but it is to be hoped that our National Councils will rely less on either than on our measures. We learn from France that Barlow is engaged in discussions which encourage his hope of doing something valuable. The return of the Hornet will enable us to form a more decided judgment. The repeal of the decrees of B. A. M. is a fact nowise in question there, though still a topic of malignant cavil here. A very large batch of the nominations for the army of 25,000 went in to the Senate to-day, and it will

soon be followed by others. General Dearborn is with us and lends a helping hand.
We are well, and offer affectionate salutations to Anna and yourself. We hope to
see you all in the spring, and that you will
pass the interim with us at Montpelier.

Yours,   JAMES MADISON.

TO ANNA.

WASHINGTON, *March* 20, 1812.

Before this reaches you, my beloved sister, Lucy will be married to Judge Todd,
of Kentucky. You are, I know, prepared
for it, and reconciled to her choice of a
man of the most estimable character.
Their home is now to be in Lexington,
very near our old friend, General Taylor,
but as a Supreme Judge he is obliged to
come here for two months every winter,
and binds himself to bring her to her
friends when she pleases to come. You
may imagine my grief is not slight at the
parting, and Lucy too is in deep distress.
. . . All are busy electioneering yet.

The Federalists affronted to a man.
Not one of the two houses of Congress
will enter Madison's door since the com-
munications of Henry except Livingston,

who considers himself attached by his appointment.

General Dearborn has had a fall, which, though not serious, confines him to the house. . . .

March 27, 1812.

The Vice-President lies dangerously ill, and electioneering for his office goes on beyond description — the world seems to be running mad, what with one thing or another. The Federalists, as I told you, were all affronted with Madison, — refused to dine with him, or even come to the house. But they have changed. Last night and the night before, our rooms were crowded with Republicans, and such a rallying of our party has alarmed them into a return. They came in a large body last night also, and are continuing calling; even D. B. W. (who is a fine fellow) came last night. The old and the young turned out together. The war business goes on slowly, but I fear it will be sure. Where are your husband's vessels? and why does he not get them in? Congress will be here until May, and perhaps longer.

TO ANNA.

WASHINGTON, 1812.

I wrote you that the Embargo would take place three or four days before it did, dear Anna. General Dearborn will leave this in a few days. I went to Mrs. Eustis's last Sunday evening with Mr. and Mrs. M. — only two or three ladies present. Foster, Serurier, General Dearborn, Mr. Brent, and one or two other men, but dull. Mrs. Hamilton and Mrs. Eustis have had parties — no one else. Congress will *not* adjourn, I believe, though it has been much spoken of ; the intention is on the decline now, from an idea that it will make a bad impression, both in and out of our country. So now, my dear sister, it seems May will smile on your journey to us; tell me when and how you begin it. I received a letter by ship from Mrs. Barlow, which I will send you. She says the Hornet will sail in a few days, and will bring us a treaty of commerce, et cetera. Every prospect is fair in that quarter.

WASHINGTON, *May* 12, 1812.

MY DEAR ANNA, — John Randolph has been firing away at the "House" this morning against the declaration of war, but we think it will have little effect. I told you of the Hornet and all the news it brought. We have nothing among ourselves worth repeating. Lucy writes often and is still delighted with Kentucky ; our friends in Virginia are all well. My dear husband is overpowered with business, but is in good health. We had all the heads of departments here yesterday to dinner, with their wives.

I will write you, dear Anna, every day that I can take up my pen, and am already prepared with a room, and every sisterly attention for your husband ; he will be here, I hope, in time to give his vote for war. However, I may be mistaken, and that dreaded epoch may be some distance off.

Payne is in Baltimore yet, and as much admired and respected as you could wish. He writes me that Mrs. Patterson and Mrs. Bonaparte are very kind to him, and he is invited out all the time. We intend

to send him in a few months to Princeton.
Kiss the sweet girls and boys for me, and
sleep in peace, my dear sister ; Heaven will
preserve you and yours as you trust in its
great power.   Ever your own

DOLLY.

Lucy Payne, who had married George
Steptoe Washington at the early age of
fifteen, was left a widow about the time
Mr. Madison entered the White House,
and lived there with them for several
years ; she then married Judge Todd, of
Kentucky, a widower, with five children,
and a man much respected by his brother
justices of the Supreme Court.   She is de-
scribed by Washington Irving, after a visit
to one of Mrs. Madison's drawing-rooms,
as bright and handsome, "reminding me
of the merry wives of Windsor."   "How
wise Lucy is," she writes, "to choose him,
in preference to the gay ones who courted
her.   Yes, my regrets are all selfish : only
for myself, not for her.   She will, I hope,
be here every winter for three months.
Mr. Madison thinks that ere long the
seven Supreme Judges may be obliged to
live at or near the seat of government."

TO MR. AND MRS. JOEL BARLOW.

WASHINGTON, *November* 15, 1811.

EVER DEAR AND VALUED FRIENDS, —
Your notes giving us an account of your
progress on the water were grateful, indeed, but the news of your safe arrival in
France infinitely more so. Many, many
are the questions that rise to my lips.
How did you bear the voyage? How is
dear Clara, Mr. Barlow, et cetera? I hope
soon to know these things, which I confess interest *me* more than the success of
your mission, of which few have a doubt.
Even the enemies of our Minister admit
his talents and virtue ; how then can any
one doubt? We passed two months on our
mountain in health and peace, returning
the first of October to a sick and afflicted
city. The unfinished canal caused a bil-
ious fever to prevail through all its
streets ; many died, and Congress con-
vened in dread of contagion. Happily all
fear is now over, and public business en-
grosses them very thoroughly. John Randolph is the only one as yet who seems
hostile to a quiet " House " They have
before them the nomination of Colonel M.

and some lesser appointments, and I believe are in a disposition to do as they are advised.

The French Minister, Mr. Serurier, is still delighted with Kalorama, and takes much pleasure in beautifying the grounds. Mrs. Baldwin was well and cheerful when I saw her some days since ; she no doubt is writing you volumes, and keeps you posted as to the health of your little dog. Mr. Madison is writing also, and will tell you that he has settled the business of the Chesapeake with Mr. Foster. I have not yet begun the journal I promised, having nothing worth relating. Mr. Barlow knows the disposition of our world better than I do, and from what I learn, good sense and principle will prevail over intrigue and vanity. You will see that Calvin declares himself the author of the boasted letters : some think this a finishing stroke, but I absolutely pity the man, — "fallen from his high estate." We have new members in abundance, with their wives and daughters ; and I have never felt the entertainment of company oppressive until now. How I wish I were in France with you for a little relaxation. As you, my dear friends, have everything and we nothing that is beautiful, I will ask the favor of you to send me by a safe vessel large head-dresses, a few flowers, feathers, gloves, and stockings, black and white, with anything else pretty, and suitable for an economist, and let me know the amount. We have a house full of company, and I must conclude with love and prayers for you all, my best friends.   Affectionately,

DOLLY MADISON.

She must have had enemies, as all persons of strong individuality are sure to have; her high-bred air and refinement, which she could not help, would hardly commend her to the average citizen, in an order of things in which mediocrity was at a premium, and her gracious presence, which rarely comes without family antecedents to account for it, "is not always agreeable," as Oliver Wendell Holmes says, "to the many, whose two ideals are the man on horseback, and the man in his shirt-sleeves." Her inordinate love of pleasing, of making every one happy about her, was called insincerity, and even "toadyism," by those who did not know the absolute pain given to the loving, faithful heart by an unkind word, or censure of herself, or the dearly loved friends, whose troubles were all taken upon her sympathetic shoulders. Having a great dislike to hot argument, or contention of any kind that might wound the feelings of others, she would quietly leave the room for a few moments, returning to find the hint taken, and peace restored. " I would rather fight with my hands than my tongue," she used to say, and indeed an atmosphere of sunshine followed her, even in the dark days during the war, when the waters of political and social life were turbid indeed, with but dim hope of clearing. Her own possessions, gowns, and the like, were at every one's disposal. "How can you think I would, or could, wear my pretty things, unless you partook," she writes to her sister Anna, who had evidently written full of the cares and responsibilities of a large family of children. " Do not give way to sad thoughts, but remember we have a goodly prospect before us of enjoying together the blessings an approving Providence has already bestowed upon us." She was devoted to children, and kept them constantly about her, replacing worn or soiled pinafores by taking them into her store-room: "Come, sweet one, and let us be tidied up," she would say; and there, with her great shears, a garment would quickly be cút out, and given to one of her women to make up. In the same way, if she thought a dress or ornament of hers could be of use to a friend, it was proffered in such a delicate manner that no feeling but gratitude could be produced.

Mr. Joel Barlow, a distinguished politician, and also something of a poet and philosopher, was sent by Mr. Madison as Minister to France, to negotiate a treaty of commerce with Napoleon, which, after many efforts failed signally. In 1812 he was invited by the Duc de Bassano to a personal conference with the Emperor in Poland, and hurrying thither in stormy weather, was seized with inflammation of the lungs and died before reaching the "rendezvous." Mrs. Madison considered him one of her warmest friends, and the correspondence between Mrs. Barlow and herself seems of the most unrestrained and affectionate character. I will add one

more letter of hers to these dear friends,
who had begged her to keep a sort of
journal, descriptive of everything that took
place in her life.

TO MR. AND MRS. JOEL BARLOW.

WASHINGTON, 1811.

This unexpected opportunity and short
notice, my beloved friends, scarce gives
me time to embrace you round; still I do
it with my whole heart. I have received
all your most welcome letters — Mr. Barlow's and Mr. Lee's, by the Constitution,
with one, too, from Mr. Warden — all of
which I should like to answer now, were
it not that the despatches go in one hour,
and I can only return to each individual
my love and best thanks for their goodness
and friendship. Before this, you know of
our Embargo, — to be followed by War!!
Yes, that terrible event is at hand, I fear;
our appointments for the purpose are
mostly made, and the recruiting business
goes on with alacrity. The major-generals are Henry Dearborn, Thomas Pinck-
ney, Joseph Bloomfield, J. Winchester,
Wm. Polk, Wm. Hull, et cetera. You will
have an account of our political situation

in all its shades by this vessel. We anticipate some little contention among ourselves on the death of the Vice-President,
whose physicians give out that he cannot
live until morning. The sentiment is in
favor of John Langdon as his successor.
Congress will remain in session, perhaps,
until July; if not, full power to declare
war will be vested in the President.

Your letters by the Neptune were particularly acceptable, as we had been worried by a report that the Emperor had
seized the Hornet, and as I promised to
write you everything, personal or imper-
sonal, you will pardon me if I say aught
that gives you pain, in preparing you for
the disappointment expressed at Mr. Barlow's having told the state of his negotiations to Mr. Granger, who directly gave it
circulation, and a place in the newspapers.
The objection to this communication is —
"that you may yet be disappointed; the
anticipations of such a treaty might cause
improper speculations;" "that Mr. G. was
not a proper channel," and much of the
same kind. All this is from the people,
not from the Cabinet, yet you know everything vibrates there.

Tell Mr. Lee that I shall be ever grateful for the fatigue and trouble he must have experienced for my sake, in procuring the valuable collection he sent me ; the bill was immediately paid, but he will be astonished at the amount of duties — two thousand dollars. I fear I shall never have money enough to send again. All the articles are beautiful ; the heads I could not get on, being a little tight, so I shall lay them aside until next winter, when I can have them enlarged to fit. The flowers, trimmings, and ornaments were enchanting. I wish I could gratify you, my dear friend, in the matter of the portraits you so kindly wish of us ; but I see little prospect at present of accomplishing it. Stuart is far from us, and we have no painter of skill in this place ; be assured, if an opportunity occurs, I will do my best to send you what you wish. My sister Lucy has gone, and Anna not yet come ; you may imagine me the very shadow of my husband. Do write me continually of your dear selves, and what you are doing ; you cannot image the impatience felt when you are silent.

Your ever affectionate

DOLLY MADISON.

Mr. Edward Coles, of Albemarle, filled the office of private secretary to Mr. Madison for six years, leaving him only to carry out a long-cherished plan of going west to Illinois, of which State he afterwards became governor. He was a cousin, and much-esteemed friend, as the following letters show.

TO MR. EDWARD COLES.

WASHINGTON, *May* 12, 1813.

Your letter caused me great affliction, my dear cousin; the continuation of your illness, and Payne's reluctance at leaving America, left me without fortitude to write, until now that a letter has come from my son on ship-board, in which he expresses satisfaction at all around him. He had seen Mr. Swertchkoff, who assured him you would soon be well in spite of yourself. We indulge this pleasing hope in addition to that of your remaining with us, to the last. Not that I would for the world retard any plan for your prosperity; but that I flatter myself the western country may be given up for something more consonant with your happiness, and that of your connections, among them

there are none who feel a more affectionate interest in you than Mr. Madison and
myself.   I hope you will believe that such
is our regard and esteem for you that we
should consider your leaving us a misfor-
tune.   Mr. Madison can do very well without a secretary until your health is reës-
tablished.   The winter is not a season for
emigration, so that next summer you will
be better able to make your election — to
go, or not to go.

And now if I could I would describe to
you the fears and alarms that circulate
around me.   For the last week all the city
and Georgetown (except the Cabinet) have
expected a visit from the enemy, and were
not lacking in their expressions of terror
and reproach.   Yesterday an express announced the pause of a frigate at the
mouth of the Potomac.   The commander
sent his boats to examine a Swedish ship
that lay near, but our informer was too
frightened to wait for further news.   We
are making considerable efforts for defense.
The fort is being repaired, and five hundred
militia, with perhaps as many regulars, are
to be stationed on the Green, near the
Windmill, or rather Major Taylor's.   The

twenty tents already look well in my eyes,
who have always been an advocate for
fighting when assailed, though a Quaker.
I therefore keep the old Tunisian sabre
within reach. One of our generals has
discovered a plan of the British, — it is to
land as many chosen rogues as they can
about fourteen miles below Alexandria, in
the night, so that they may be on hand to
burn the President's house and offices. I
do not tremble at this, but feel hurt that
the admiral (of Havre de Grace memory)
should send me word that he would make
his bow at my drawing-room very soon.
Mrs. Buonaparte and Miss Stevenson returned to their house four days ago to
secure their wardrobe, but I question
whether they leave us again, as strangers
and members are crowding in. Mr. Monroe and family dined with us yesterday in
a large party given to Mr. Jones. Mr.
Hay is with them, having come to escort
Mrs. Monroe to Richmond on a visit of
three weeks to her two daughters. Cousin
Sally is still in South Carolina, and Miss
Mayo is as gay as ever. Anna has not
been very well of late, and her children
are ill with measles, so that I confine myself very much with them.

Be careful of yourself, dear cousin, and return as soon as you can to your anxious friends.   DOLLY MADISON.

WASHINGTON, *June* 10, 1813.

Mr. Madison has received your letter, my dear cousin, and desires me to answer "as I please" the subject of his picture; when I will take advantage of the occasion to express my great sorrow at the cause of your detention, and my hope that you will exert great fortitude, knowing that a cheerful spirit will aid your recovery. By the Ida I received a letter from dear Payne. He is charmed with his voyage so far, and had escaped sea-sickness, though all the party had succumbed. You will pity me, I know, when you hear that Mitchell has left us for France, that I am acting in his department, and that the city is so full of strangers I am positively dizzy. There is so much to say to you and so little time. About the picture, if Mr. D. will return it safe in six months, more or less, he may send for it as soon as ever he chooses. Present me to Dr. Physic, and pray tell P. Morris that I love her as much as ever. Yours in friendship,
DOLLY P. MADISON.

July 2, 1813.

I have the happiness to assure you, my dear cousin, that Mr. Madison recovers; for the last three weeks his fever has been so slight as to permit him to take bark every hour and with good effect. It is three weeks now I have nursed him, night and day, — sometimes with despair! but now that I see he will get well I feel as if I might die myself from fatigue. Adieu!

Ever yours,   D. P. MADISON.

TO GOVERNOR COLES, ILLINOIS.

MONTPELIER, *September* 5, 1819.

I am afraid, dear cousin, that while you and I deliberate who to choose for a wife, we shall lose some of the finest girls now grown. For instance, it is reported that Ellen Randolph is to be married to General Cooke, and Virginia to William Burwell. Our niece Eliza was married to Mr. Willis in May, and his sister is to be bound to her brother on the 16th of this month; still I have hopes for you, that your future one may become manifest to reward your merits and long search.

We have been expecting a visit from my

beloved Sally, until within the last few days, when I was informed she had gone to the Virginia Springs. Payne still says he will write to you. I suspect he begins to feel with you that a good wife would add to his happiness. I am sadly disappointed at not having my dear Lucy with me next winter; the Judge has persuaded her to remain in Frankfort until they can remove altogether, which the change in the judiciary will soon authorize him to do. We have now with us a visitor from Washington, the curious Captain O'Brion; he tells us a medley of news, blended with sea-phrases, which, to appreciate, you must hear. The President passed a day with us on his return to the city, and looked much better than was expected after his fatigues. Mr. Madison has gone with him to Loudon. I must not expect to amuse you, only in truth can assure you of our affectionate interest and friendship, hoping to see you soon amongst us.

DOLLY P. MADISON.

CHAPTER VIII.

THE first three years of Mrs. Madison's life in the White House were passed in unclouded peacc and happiness; a prosperity, however, which was doomed. Insatiate warriors already surrounded the peace-loving, humane Madison, urging him to take decisive steps against Great Britain. He had no disposition, and but little capacity, for war, and his various messages to Congress were marked as the productions of a ruler rather too cautious to suit the fiery leaders of the Democracy, who supported the President's administration ; and notwithstanding the opposition of the Federalists, the war-spirit fired the popular heart.

On the 4th of April, 1812, an Act was passed by Congress laying an Embargo for ninety days on all British vessels within the jurisdiction of the United States. On June 4th the President sent an able and conclusive message to Congress, urging

war as the only means of once more as-
serting our independence.   The resolution
passed both the House and Senate, and
vigorous preparations were made for the im-
pending conflict.   The 18th of June, 1812,
is memorable to every one as the beginning of that three years' war whose fierce-
ness was felt from Canada to New Orleans.
It will not be necessary to go into the de-
tails of our brave fight with an incredibly
small navy, where personal heroism seemed
to take the place of numbers.   From the
first it became evident that the war was
destined to be a conflict on the sea coast
and the ocean, the condition of both nations
being such as to provoke this sort of warfare, and the many daring deeds are familiar
to us, both in prose and song.   After the
Revolution, especially during the administration of Jefferson, the military spirit was
discouraged, and the defenses fell into de-
cay.   Upon a few scattered fortifications
and the terror inspired by Fulton's torpe-
does, the Americans must depend for the
defense of a coast-line reaching from Pas-
samaquoddy to the St. Mary's.   Great,
therefore, was the astonishment of the
world when the American sailors took the

initiative, and with great alacrity, and without a tremor, set forth to smite the mistress of the seas. And greater the admiration when a series of brilliant victories declared for the flag of the Republic, and the navy of the United States won a just and lasting renown. At this critical time, 1813, Madison entered upon his second term of Presidency, and the choice of Vice-President fell upon Elbridge Gerry, of Massachusetts. Mr. Jefferson, gazing out upon the world from his retirement at Monticello, writes again to a friend (Thomas Flournoy) of his great confidence in his successor : —

" Servile inertness is not what is wanted to save our country. The conduct of a war requires the vigor and enterprise of younger heads, and therefore all such undertakings are out of the question with me, and I say so with the greater satisfaction, when I contemplate the person to whom the powers were handed over. You probably may not know Mr. Madison personally, or at least intimately, as I do. I have known him from 1779, when he first came into the public councils ; and from three and thirty years' trials, I can say conscientiously that I do not know a man in the world of purer integrity, more disinterested and devoted to genuine Republicanism, than himself, nor could I, in the whole scope of America and Europe, point out an abler head. He may be illy seconded by others, betrayed by the Hulls and Arnolds of our country, for such there are everywhere, we know only too well. But what man can do will be done by Mr. Madison. I hope, therefore, there will be no difference among Republicans as to his reëlection, for we shall only appreciate his true value when we have to give him up, and look at large for a successor."

The American army was now organized in three divisions : The army of the north, commanded by General Wade Hampton, to operate in the country of Lake Champlain ; the army of the centre, under the direction of the Commander-in-chief, to resume offensive movements on the Niagara frontier and Lake Ontario ; the army of the west, under command of General Winchester, who was soon superseded by General Harrison. Many battles were fought both on land and sea, and much blood and treasure wasted ; but the year closed with

out decisive results. Late in the. summer
of the year 1814, Admiral Cockburn arrived off the coast of Virginia with an ar-
mament of twenty-one vessels. General
Ross, with an army of four thousand vet-
erans, freed from service in Europe, came
with the fleet. The American squadron,
commanded by Commodore Barney, was
unable to oppose so powerful a force, and
the enemy's flotilla entered the Chesapeake
with the purpose of attacking Washington
and Baltimore. Commodore Barney was
obliged to leave his ships and take to the
shore, meeting the British troops with a
small band of undisciplined militia at Bladensburg, where a battle was fought, and
he himself taken prisoner.

Mrs. Madison's course during all this
time was one of peace, her great effort
being to destroy, as far as her power lay,
the bitter feeling between Federalists and
Republicans. Women, as usual, took ex-
aggerated views of politics, and one (who
afterwards changed her politics and apolo-
gized) drove to Mrs. Madison's door, and
standing up in her carriage, loosened her
beautiful hair, which was celebrated for its
length, praying that she might have the

privilege of parting with it, for the purpose
of hanging Mr. Madison. A week before
the British entered the city of Washington, Mr. Monroe, the Secretary of State,
mounted his horse, and rode to Benedict, a
small village on the Patuxent, and there
sadly witnessed the landing of the enemy
on our shores. Knowing how unprepared
was the seat of government for defense, he
instantly ordered the public papers and
records in his department to be removed
and placed in some safe spot, which was
accordingly done by Mr. Pleasanton, a
clerk. A large number of linen bags were
made, which, filled with papers, were conveyed in carts and wagons to Leesburg,
about thirty-five miles from Washington,
and placed in an empty house, just in time
to see the flames arising from the burning
of the government buildings. The English used many stratagems to gain possession of Mr. Madison's papers. Spies found
their way into his house, disguised as women. Anonymous letters were received
threatening his life with the dagger or poi-
son. All remained unheeded until the
English officer, in command of the advancing troops, sent word to Mrs. Madison

that unless she should leave, the house
would be burned over her head.

Generous British sentiments revolted at
the destruction of the American capital,
but it was impossible to satisfy warfare, in
its abominable lust for libraries, buildings,
objects of art, and embodiments of national
pride. The day before the fall of Washington was one of extreme alarm ; the Secretary of State wrote to the President:
" The enemy has advanced six miles along
the road to the wood-yard, and our troops
are retreating. You had better make all
preparations to leave." Then began the
panic, which was doomed to grow more
intense, as hour after hour passed on.
Scarcely had the wagons that bore the
papers crossed the wooden bridge over the
Potomac, than crowds of fugitive women
and children pressed upon it, in such numbers as to render the present danger even
greater than the one they were fleeing from.
The frightened multitude swayed to and fro,
seeking means of escape, till night closed
in upon the horrible drama ; then, upon
Capitol Hill, appeared the red-coated soldiery of the British army. The sun sank
peacefully behind the bank of fleecy clouds

that floated softly over the southern hori-
zon, contrasting with the terrible atmosphere below.   Dust and heat were intolerable, and a rumor that the water was
poisoned rendered the sufferings of the
weary soldiers painful in the extreme.   For
the seventh time that day a retreat was
commanded, and the city troops, mortified
and enraged, refused at first to obey.   Back
from the city to the heights of Georgetown
was the order ; to leave their families, their
homes, and property behind them, march-
ing away from those they were sworn to
protect.   Down the long, broad, solitary
avenue, past the President's house, through
Georgetown, and even as far as Tennally-
town, the demoralized, disorganized rem-
nant of the army wended their weary way,
resting on the ground lighted up by the
fiery red glare from the burning buildings
in Washington.   All through that terrible
night they lay in the fields, too frightened
and miserable to steal more than a few
moments' sleep.   The bursting shells in
the navy yard were heard for miles, each
boom sounding a knell to the agonized
hearts, all ignorant of the fate of dear
friends during those hours of horror and

darkness. When the British marched
slowly into the deserted city by the lurid
light that shot up from the blazing Capitol, the population had dwindled down to
a few stragglers, and the slaves of the
absent residents. The houses scattered
over a large space were closed, and no sign
of life visible. Mr. Madison had crossed
the Potomac early in the afternoon, and
his wife had gone in another direction.
The bayonets of the British gleamed as
they filed down the avenue, and the fulmi-
nations from the navy yard saluted them
as they passed. Nothing but the prayers
and entreaties of the women and the ex-
postulations of the residents deterred the
British commander, General Ross, from
blowing up the Capitol; he contented himself, however, by firing it at all points, and
destroying with it many houses in the vicinity, among which was one belonging to
General Washington. "I have, indeed,
to this hour [said Mr. Bush in 1855] the
vivid impression upon my eye of columns
of smoke and flame ascending all through
the night of August 24, 1814, from the
Capitol, President's house, and other public buildings, as the whole were on fire,

some burning slowly, others with bursts of flames, and sparks mounting high in the dark heavens. This can never be forgotten by me, as I accompanied on that memorable night President Madison, Mr. Jones, Secretary of the Navy, General Mason, of Anacostia Island, and Mr. Carroll, of Bellevue, across the river. If, at intervals, the heart-breaking sight was lost to our view, we found it again from some hill-top or eminence, where we would pause to gaze at it." Among the many stories which greeted Congress, when it met near the ruins some three weeks afterward, was that Admiral Cockburn, in a strain of coarse levity, mounting the Speaker's chair in the Capitol, went through the form of putting the question: "Shall this harbor of Yankee democracy be burned?" And when the mock resolution was declared unanimous, it was carried into effect, by placing combustibles under the furniture. The temporary wooden structure readily ignited; doors, chairs, the library, and its contents in an upper room of the senate wing, everything that could burn, soon disappeared in sheets of flame, illuminating the country for thirty miles around.

Through the " eternal Pennsylvania Avenue," the British commanders led their
elated troops, where, but a few hours
before, the flying, scattered Americans,
ashamed and despairing, had wended their
sorrowful way, the Capitol behind them,
wrapt in its winding robe of flame. At a
house near the President's mansion they
halted and ordered supper, which was
eaten by General Ross and Admiral Cockburn, in the glare of their own barbarous
handiwork. This onslaught was so unexpected that a dinner-party had been arranged by Mrs. Madison for that day, and
the following note from Mrs. Jones, wife
of the Secretary of the Navy, shows that
though surprised and alarmed, they even
then had no idea of immediate danger : —

TO MRS. MADISON.

WASHINGTON, *August* 23, 1814.

MY DEAR MADAM, — In the present
state of alarm and bustle of preparation
for the worst that may happen, I imagine
it will be more convenient to dispense
with the enjoyment of your hospitality to-
day, and, therefore, pray you to admit this
as an excuse for Mr. Jones, Lucy, and

myself. Mr. Jones is deeply engaged in dispatching the marines and attending to other public duties. Lucy and I are packing, with the possibility of having to leave; but in the event of necessity we know not where to go, nor have we any means yet prepared for the conveyance of our effects. I sincerely hope and trust the necessity may be avoided, but there appears rather serious cause of apprehension. Our carriage horse is sick, and our coachman absent, or I should have called last evening to see your sister. I feel great solicitude on her account. Yours very truly and affectionately,   E. JONES.

Hoping and fearing, Mrs. Madison lingered on at the President's house for Mr. Madison's return, until the British officers were actually at the threshold, and the moment could be no longer delayed. She had secured the public papers and the Declaration of Independence, and was being hurried out to the waiting carriage by Mr. De Peyster and Mr. Barker, when her eye was attracted by the valuable portrait of General Washington hanging on the wall, this being one of the few adornments

of the White House at that time, and an
excellent likeness of the adored first President. She felt she could not leave it, and at
the risk of capture herself, resolved to save
it, if possible. After much valuable time
spent in trying to unfasten the great frame
from the wall, the servants were obliged to
break the outside edge with an axe, keeping the entire canvas, however, quite unin-
jured ; this they sent in a hack to a woman
named Baker, living beyond Georgetown.
The portrait was painted partly by Gilbert
Stuart, and completed by Winstanley, with
Colonel Smith, the son-in-law of President
John Adams, as a model for the unfinished body and limbs. Half a century later,
when the White House was being rebuilt,
this picture was renovated and put back in
its place on the wall, together with many
others added to the collection. " I lived a
lifetime in those last moments," she tells
a friend afterwards, " waiting for Madison's
return, and in an agony of fear lest he
might have been taken prisoner ! Anna,
too, was away, I hardly knew where."
Fortunately her mind was in a measure relieved by meeting Mr. Madison, who, with
several friends, had come back to see after

her safety.   She insisted upon going with
him to the Virginia shore, and then, and
not until then, did she yield to the persua-
sions of her friends, and seek rest in the
house of an acquaintance, about two miles
beyond Georgetown.   Sleep, of course, was
impossible, and the long night was passed
at the window, gazing at the flames, which
looked as if nothing could stop them in
their mad fury.

A letter written to her sister the day
before gives an insight into her feelings
at this time of trial and danger.

TO ANNA.

Tuesday, August 23, 1814.

Dear Sister, — My husband left me
yesterday morning to join General Win-
der.   He inquired anxiously whether I
had courage or firmness to remain in the
President's house until his return on the
morrow, or succeeding day, and on my assurance that I had no fear but for him,
and the success of our army, he left, be-
seeching me to take care of myself, and
of the Cabinet papers, public and private.
I have since received two despatches from
him, written with a pencil.   The last is

alarming, because he desires I should be ready at a moment's warning to enter my carriage, and leave the city ; that the enemy seemed stronger than had at first been reported, and it might happen that they would reach the city with the intention of destroying it. I am accordingly ready ; I have pressed as many Cabinet papers into trunks as to fill one carriage ; our private property must be sacrificed, as it is impossible to procure wagons for its transportation. I am determined not to go myself until I see Mr. Madison safe, so that he can accompany me, as I hear of much hostility towards him. Disaffection stalks around us. My friends and acquaintances are all gone, even Colonel C. with his hundred, who were stationed as a guard in this inclosure. French John (a faithful servant), with his usual activity and resolution, offers to spike the cannon at the gate, and lay a train of powder, which would blow up the British, should they enter the house. To the last proposition I positively object, without being able to make him understand why all advantages in war may not be taken.

Wednesday Morning, twelve o'clock. —

Since sunrise I have been turning my spy-glass in every direction, and watching with unwearied anxiety, hoping to discover the approach of my dear husband and his friends ; but, alas ! I can descry only groups of military, wandering in all directions, as if there was a lack of arms, or of spirit to fight for their own fireside.

Three o'clock. — Will you believe it, my sister ? we have had a battle, or skirmish, near Bladensburg, and here I am still, within sound of the cannon ! Mr. Madison comes not. May God protect us ! Two messengers, covered with dust, come to bid me fly ; but here I mean to wait for him. . . . At this late hour a wagon has been procured, and I have had it filled with plate and the most valuable portable articles, belonging to the house. Whether it will reach its destination, the " Bank of Maryland," or fall into the hands of British soldiery, events must determine. Our kind friend, Mr. Carroll, has come to hasten my departure, and in a very bad humor with me, because I insist on waiting until the large picture of General Washington is secured, and it requires to be unscrewed from the wall. This process was found too tedious for these perilous moments; I have ordered the frame to be broken, and the canvas taken out. It is done! and the precious portrait placed in the hands of two gentlemen of New York, for safe keeping. And now, dear sister, I must leave this house, or the retreating army will make me a prisoner in it by filling up the road I am directed to take. When I shall again write to you, or where I shall be to-morrow, I cannot tell!   DOLLY.

John Sioussa, the French porter, was the last to leave the house, and after seeing Mrs. Madison safely off, he took a macaw, which had been much petted by her, to the house of a friend, Colonel Taylor; then locking the house carefully, he deposited the key with the Russian Minister, Mr. Dashoff, whose house was protected by his country's flag, and went to Philadelphia. All the afternoon, parties of straggling soldiers, on their way to Georgetown, with vagrant negroes pilfered in many directions, in spite of the efforts of faithful servants. Mad with disappointment at the escape of the President and his wife, "whom they wanted to capture and show in England," the enemy broke open the doors of the White House, and ransacked it from cellar to attic, finding nothing of value, in the way of trophies, except a small bundle of pencil notes received by Mrs. Madison from her husband when he was with the troops, and which she had inadvertently rolled together, and left in her table drawer. To everything else in the house, furniture, wines, provisions, and family stores of all kinds, which had cost Mr. Madison twelve thousand dollars, together with an excellent library, the torch was applied. Fire for the purpose was procured at a small beer-house opposite the Treasury, and common soldiers, together with negroes, and thieves of all grades, did what they could to pillage and destroy. The White House was not so large and complete as it is now. The east room, which had served Mrs. Adams for a drying-room, was bare and unfurnished; the whole house was plain, unfinished, and totally destitute of ornament; the front vestibule had not then been added, and the grounds were uninclosed, and entirely uncultivated.

Nothing but the lateness of the hour

and the threatening storm prevented the troops from firing the War Department. The promised reinforcement had failed to come, filling the minds of the officers with vague and timorous apprehension, and they resolved to evacuate the next day. Constant rumors and frights had unnerved the stoutest hearts, and the unhappy citizens of Washington flying from a foreign foe rendered the situation of those who could not leave even more distressing. All the vehicles had been pressed into the service, and valuables scattered in every direction for safety.

An English narrator states that "the most tremendous hurricane ever remembered by the inhabitants broke over Washington the day after the conflagration. Roofs of houses were torn off and carried up into the air like sheets of paper, while the rain which accompanied it was like the rushing of a mighty cataract rather than the dropping of a shower. This lasted for two hours without intermission, during which time many of the houses spared by us were blown down, and thirty of our men, with as many more of the inhabitants, were buried beneath the ruins.

Two cannons standing upon a bit of rising ground were fairly lifted in the air and carried several yards to the rear."

Long before day Mrs. Madison and her sleepless companions bade farewell to their hospitable friend and started forth to the place appointed by Mr. Madison for a meeting. Consternation and despair were at their height; the whole region filled with frightened people and straggling soldiers, roaming about and spreading alarms that the enemy was coming now this way, now that, making no place safe. As the day wore on the storm burst upon the forlorn refugees, as they traveled slowly, and with great difficulty, through roundabout lanes and roads to the little tavern in the middle of an apple orchard, sixteen miles from Washington, where Mr. Madison had promised to join them. Here the drenched, tired travelers were very inhospitably received; the house was crowded with refugees, who, frightened and miserable, worked themselves up into a feeling of anger and reproach against Mr. Madison and herself, declaring them to be the cause of their present troubles, and refusing them entrance. With evening came another furious thunder-storm, and common humanity made them open the doors to the poor shivering women, who were afraid to leave the neighborhood for fear of missing their friends. The sky was as black as night, and the thunder and lightning seemed almost continuous : at one time striking a tree in the woods near by, at another flashing into the dark little waiting-room, lighting up the faces of the awed and panic-stricken women, who had passed through so much in this last twenty-four hours. Slowly the hours dragged on, the storm abated, but the anxious wife looked in vain for her husband. Nervous and intensely anxious, Mrs. Madison waited on in breathless impatience for the promised relief, too unhappy to feel the discomforts around her ; until late in the night her fears were relieved by the approach of Mr. Madison with the friends who had accompanied him the night before. He looked careworn and weary, and after a somewhat scant meal of such food as had been left in the over-crowded tavern, he yielded to his wife's entreaties and sought forgetfulness in sleep.

During that time General Ross hastily

evacuated the town ; victors and vanquished alike victims of imaginary perils :
the one superstitiously fearful of the violent, almost tropical, storms to which they
were unused, and credulous of vague reports of reinforcements on the other side ;
while the American troops were still too
scattered and frightened to distinguish the
false from the true in the rumors of mur-
der and rapine that were flying in all directions.

Toward midnight a courier, breathless
from fatigue and excitement, warned the
President that the enemy had discovered
a clue to his hiding-place, and were even
now on their way hither. Yielding to the
entreaties of his wife and friends he sought
refuge in a miserable little hovel in the
woods, where the boughs moaned and
sobbed around him, and the storm ex-
pended itself in dismal sighs through the
tall trees ; here he spent the remainder of
the night, expecting at any moment to
hear the tread of the British solidiers as
they passed, or perhaps halted and searched
for the coveted prisoner.

Mrs. Madison had promised to disguise
herself and seek safety further on ; so at-

tended only by Mr. Duvall and one soldier she started out at the first dawn of day, leaving her carriage to her companions and taking a small wagon. Before they had gone very far, however, the news reached them that Washington was evacuated, and joyfully retracing their steps, after a weary ride they reached the Long Bridge, only to find it burned at both ends. Forgetting her disguises he appealed to an officer standing by to take her across the river in the one remaining boat, but was curtly refused, not daring, as he said, "to let an unknown woman into the city." No alternative was left but to explain who she was, and after some doubt and demur on his part the frail little craft landed them safely on the other side. There she found her former home in ruins, and the smoke still rising from the heaps of blackened timber that greeted her on every side ; the streets were as deserted and quiet as the forests through which she had just passed, and sick at heart she turned away, and in a strange carriage drove to the house of her sister, Mrs. Cutts, to await the return of Mr. Madison.

"The memory of the burning of Wash·

ington cannot be obliterated. It can never be thought of by an American, and ought not to be thought of by an enlightened Englishman, except with deplorable shame and mortification. History cannot record it as a trophy of war for a great nation. The metropolis at that time had the aspect of a straggling village, interspersed here and there by a handsome public building, and with a scattered population of not more than eight thousand inhabitants; fortresses there were none, and but a few mounted cannon."

Late in the day, the news reached the President in his hovel that the enemy had retreated to their shipping; and he, too, turned his steps toward the city and rejoined his wife.

CHAPTER IX.

FROM the beginning many of the people of New England had opposed the war. Their interests centred in ships and factories; the former were at sea, and the latter came to a stand-still. Industry was paralyzed, and the members of the Federal party cried out against a continuance of the contest. A convention was called, which assembled at Hartford, and ruined the Federal party. Meanwhile many battles were fought on sea and land, and hostilities lingered on until the spring of 1814. American commissioners were sent to Ghent, in Belgium, and were there met by the British ambassadors. The agents of the United States were John Quincy Adams, James A. Bayard, Henry Clay, Jonathan Russell, and Albert Gallatin. Several months were spent in negotiations; and on the 24th of December, 1814, a treaty was agreed to and signed, which was received in England with deep satis-

faction, and in America with a delight
bordering on madness. Before the terms
of settlement could be made known, the
people broke forth in universal jubilee,
nobody stopping to inquire whether the
treaty was good or bad, honorable or dis-
honorable. Nor could the country be
blamed for rejoicing that a conflict which
had cost the United States one thousand
six hundred and eighty-three vessels, and
more than eighteen thousand sailors, was
ended. The war-cloud rolled away from
the public mind, and immediately the dock
yards were ringing with the sound of saw
and hammer. On the 18th of February
the treaty was ratified by the Senate of
the United States, and peace was publicly
proclaimed ; not soon enough, however, to
prevent the terrible bloodshed at the battle of New Orleans, which occurred in
the interim between the conclusion of the
treaty and the reception of the news in
America. Deeply in debt as the country
was, her monetary affairs in a deplorable
condition, and domestic commerce at a
stand-still, one advantage had been gained
by America, the recognition of her naval
power. It was no longer doubtful that

American sailors were the peers in valor
and patriotism of any seamen in the world.
It was no small triumph for the Republic
that her flag should henceforth be honored
on every ocean. Political troubles having
become partially straightened out in 1814,
Mr. and Mrs. Madison retired to Montpelier for a month or two to recruit, and
rest body and mind after the great excitement so recently undergone. Here it was
that two old Quaker ladies, Rebecca
Hubbs and Sarah Scull, members of her
society in Philadelphia in years gone by,
came to pay a visit, not only of affection,
but perhaps with a little curiosity, to ascer-
tain if the adulation and worldly life of so
many years had corrupted the heart and
mind of their much-loved sister ; and that
they were satisfied is shown from the following letter from Rebekah Hubbs on her
return.

TO MRS. MADISON.

Seventh Month, 13, 1814.

DEAR FRIEND, — Thinking it may be
acceptable I put pen to paper to write thee
a few lines, in part to inform thee of the
manner in which we got along and my safe

return home. The kind reception we met with when at thy dwelling has caused my mind to be much with thee and thine. Since we parted from thee particularly so, dear Dorothy, for several days after, when at a clear, flowing brook, with the help of thy kindness, we poor pilgrims were refreshed on the way, which seemed to satisfy as a sit meal at a full spread table; and though we were strangers in a strange land, yet at times were enabled to rejoice that the Lord had counted us worthy to suffer shame for his sake. We were favored to get along very well, and arrived at Baltimore the day preceding the yearly meeting, where I received a letter from home, and was informed that my dear babe was ill and by account could not expect to recover.

The next day after this news my beloved companion, Sarah Scull, was taken sick. This centred my mind in deep humility before the Lord, and thankful of my own health, desirous that every trying dispensation may be prosperous in their errand to me, I endeavored to resign my will to the Divine will, and parting with my companion in good hands at Baltimore, set out for home, where through the protection of Divine mercy I found my husband and children in good health, and my dear babe recovered of her sickness. And now, my dear friend, having visited thy dwelling much bowed down in mind under a sense of my weakness, having none but the Lord to appeal to, to justify me in my visit, to relieve my mind of much that was on it. Dear friend, thou hast a precious talent committed to thy trust by the King of kings, and my soul's desire for thee is that thou may more and more come out of all that cumbers the earth, and redeem thy soul from all difficulties that do or may attend it. My wishes for thee and thine is that thou may be supported under every exercise of mind, and witness the living presence of Jesus Christ, to war against vanity, pleasure, ambition, and avarice, and to put from thee all the fading pleasures of this world, but rather prize the crown immortal that fadeth not away. Assuredly, dear Dorothy, I think I shall ever remember thee with gratitude of heart, thee and thy beloved companion, your kind and Christian entertainment of us ; God will not be wanting to reward

your love.   Desirous to be had in remembrance by thee, dear Dorothy, in love, I
conclude, and remain thy soul's best
wisher,   REBEKAH HUBBS.

My love to thy dear, ancient mother-in-
law, who I believe is not far from the
kingdom of Heaven.   Sarah Scull joins
in that love which neither time nor distance can erase.

A letter from the postmaster at New
Orleans, written on the 19th of January, to
Mrs. Madison, announces the departure of
the British troops from our shores at last.
He evidently was desirous of being the
first to break the joyful news to one who
would sympathize so heartily with the
people's delight.

NEW ORLEANS, *January* 19, 1815.
MRS. MADISON :
MADAM, — I had confidently hoped from
the events of the last fourteen days to have
announced to you in this letter the departure from our shores of the implacable
foe, who, trusting to our supposed disun-
ion and disaffection, has had the temerity

to assail us at our very thresholds ; but although he still maintains a precarious foothold on our soil, be assured, madam, he speedily must abandon it, covered with disgrace.

Madam, the American army in Louisiana has gained immortal glory. It has made a defense against the most valiant and fortunate troops of Europe, excited to desperation by resistance, and staking its all of reputation on the die, unsurpassed in the annals of military warfare, its leader achieving in one hour the object of a whole campaign, — the preservation of the state from conquest, and the overthrow of its invaders. The 8th of January will form an epoch in the history of the Republic. It was on the morning of that day the British, led on by Mr. Edward Packenham, attempted to storm our lines, and to force a way to the city at the point of the bayonet. Advancing in full confidence with this intent, and encouraged to it by their commander, his watchword " booty and beauty," they were suffered to approach within twenty yards of our batteries unmolested, at which moment a fire from our guns and our musketry opened on them with such irresistible force, they gave way at all points, flying in the utmost confusion, leaving the ground strewn with their dead and dying.

You may conceive, madam, what a spectacle of carnage must have met the eye, after the battle, when you learn that in killed, wounded, and missing, the loss of the enemy exceeded two thousand ; eight hundred being left dead ; their commander - in - chief killed ; Generals Gibbs and Keene severely wounded, and the flower of their army, the 4th and the 21st regiments, almost exterminated. On the other side of the river we were momentarily dispossessed of a battery by the enemy (the guns of which, however, we had time to spike), in consequence of a part of our troops being seized with a panic, in spite of the better countenance maintained by their comrades to the last, and the exhortations of their officers not to dishonor themselves. But it was attended with a further disaster, Colonel Thornton retreating almost immediately, badly wounded.

12 o'clock. — Intelligence has at this moment been received from General Jackson that the British have evacuated the coun-

try. The rear of their army completed the
retreat to their shipping last night, leaving behind them many of their men, des-
perately wounded, besides several pieces
of cannon. The city is in a ferment of delight. The country is saved, the enemy
vanquished, and hardly a widow or an orphan whose tears damp the general joy.
All is exultation and jubilee. What do
we not owe a protecting Providence for
this manifestation of his favor! Permit
me to offer you my congratulations on this
auspicious termination of our trials and
tribulations, and to assure you of the ever-
lasting respect of

Your obedient and admiring servant,

THOMAS B. JOHNSON.

Mrs. Madison's only child, James Payne
Todd, the son of her first marriage, had
been educated at an excellent Roman
Catholic school in Baltimore, under the
charge of the Bishop of Maryland. Having a fortune in his own right, and being
the idol of his mother, he had grown up
rather self-willed and impatient of control,
though bright and attractive; so much so
that it was proposed he should be attached

to the special embassy going to Ghent to confer with the British representatives on the subject of the famous treaty. This offer was immediately accepted by Mrs. Madison for her son, knowing that going with her cordial friends would insure every kindness to the young man, while the life with them, in Washington, brought with it many temptations. The following two letters from Mrs. Albert Gallatin were found among Mrs. Madison's papers, giving tidings of the absent son.

NEW YORK, *July* 2, 1814.

I understand, my dear friend, that you did not receive any letter from Payne by the last arrivals. I will communicate to you with pleasure what Mr. Gallatin says of him. He says Todd and Millegan left St. Petersburg before them, and took the Sweden route; found the coast frozen, and after a long detention came by way of Copenhagen, and joined them at Amsterdam the day before they left it; that Payne had gone on a visit to Paris, and was to return to Mr. Gallatin in three weeks; he set off the 7th of May from London. He will have a very pleasant jaunt, no doubt, and Dallas expected to follow him. Mille-gan was gone on a message to Gotten-burgh. I dare not write you a long letter for fear of being too late for the mail, and I wish you to get the information as soon as possible, for I know you must be anx-ious. Remember me to your sister, and believe me your very sincere friend,

H. GALLATIN.

NEW YORK, *August* 13, 1815.

Ah, my dear friend, what misery are we enduring! How can Mr. Crawford be so unfeeling? I thought you had certainly received every information about your be-loved Payne, and was in hopes from day to day that it would come to Mr. C.'s recol-lection, also, what my feelings must be. But alas! not one word from him. William Nicholson (whom you may remember lived with us) tells me that Mr. Crawford wrote to Mr. Gallatin that the ship could not be detained on account of Mr. Bayard, and that Mr. Gallatin answered it was impos-sible for them to be at Plymouth before the 24th of June, and that they sailed im-mediately without waiting for any further information from them. It is proved, to be sure, that there was no time to be lost, for poor Mr. Bayard died the sixth day after their arrival. Mr. Crawford I can never forgive for not attending a little to our feelings. Oh! what anguish there is in disappointed hope. Our servant, Henry, has arrived in the Neptune with all Mr. Gallatin's and James's baggage; I have written to Captain Jones to send them on here to me with Henry, who is a faithful, excellent creature. His family live in Washington, and I presume he will be anxious to go and see them. I will then get him to take charge of all the things belonging to Payne and yourself, and deliver them in Washington. I am told he was much distressed at the ship's sailing without his master.

I have seen in the newspaper that a vessel had arrived at Boston, direct from London, left there the 26th of June, and the captain says was to have brought out Messrs. Clay, Gallatin, and suite, but they afterwards concluded to sail from Liverpool. I presume from this that they had finished the treaty, and we may expect them any moment. I think they will come to New York, and the instant they arrive, my dear friend, I will let you know of it. You and I can best feel for one another. In the mean time, if Mr. Crawford should give you any information about them, do let me know ; at all events, write to me, like a dear friend. I believe the captain on board is careful, and we need not feel uneasy about our properties ; but what a disappointment to those left behind, — all the clothes they needed at sea, besides little conveniences which will be hard for my poor husband, who is distressedly sick at sea, and Henry was his nurse. I can neither eat nor sleep, after all my anxiety about the Neptune, that she should arrive without my husband and child. It is, indeed, distressing beyond anything, and I fear to expect them, lest I should have another disappointment. It must be a comfort to you to have your sister with you, and it is a pleasure to me to hear that she and her children are well. Pray remember me to her, and to Mr. Madison. Heaven bless you.

Ever your affectionate friend,

H. GALLATIN.

TO MRS. MADISON FROM MADAME D'YRUJO
(SALLY McKEAN).

BALTIMORE, *June* 20, 1812.

My dear Mrs. Madison, — I arrived
here about ten days ago, and had a strong
desire to write you the moment of my arrival, but the state of affairs suggested to
me this idea, that it was most prudent to
suspend it until things took a decisive turn,
lest some exalted patriot might suspect
our innocent correspondence. This motive
having at present ceased, I do not lose a
moment to write you; it would delight me
to spend a day with you, and be able to
press you to my heart, but I am obliged to
set out for Philadelphia to-morrow, or next
day, at furthest. I will not leave America,
however, without seeing you. On account
of the Marquis's health becoming affected
by the climate of Brazil, he asked to be
recalled, and we were on the point of embarking in a ship going directly to Spain,
when, happily for me, a fine ship from this
port came along, and I prevailed on the
Marquis to return by way of my own dear
native country, on condition of departing
for Cadiz in October. But I will not go
before next spring, if I can possibly help it,
for am tired of so many long voyages.

Your son Payne has been twice to see me, but unfortunately I was out both times; the Marquis saw him, and says he is a fine young man, grown so tall and handsome. I shall make an effort to find him to-day, and intend to ask him if he remembers that when a little fellow he pulled off General Van Courtland's wig at the very moment he was making me a flourishing compliment. What has become of the old beau? The ladies and gentlemen of this place have been very polite to me, every one has been to see us, and I have dined at home but once.

I have been highly amused by a piece of poetry, relative to a scene they say took place in Washington last winter, in which the famous Count de Crillon cut a figure, as well as some ladies, and I am told the winter was a most dashing one in your city. I am sorry the Count P. left just before our arrival, so many fine things are said in his praise. I find Madame Bonaparte a good deal changed. We had heard in Rio Janeiro that she bore the title of "Duchess," and had a salary of fifty thousand pounds. I verily think when I see you and Anna once more, there is

so much to tell you of what I have seen
and heard abroad as would keep me talking
for three days without stopping, and I am
morally certain I should make you laugh,
and your good husband too, for I am just
as giddy and full of spirits as ever. Indeed, I am for the French principle, never
to let anything trouble me much unless it
is absolutely necessary.

Your sister Lucy is again married, I
hear, but am sorry she has gone so far off ;
rumor says she has been a great belle, and
is as lively and amiable as ever. Tell me
if you received a letter from me dated Rio
Janeiro, by Mr. C. of this place, as I never
received an answer. In answer to the thousand questions I have asked about you,
they say that you never looked so well in
your life, and that you give and have given
universal satisfaction to all friends and
visitors, which is, indeed, a very difficult
matter, that of pleasing everybody. You,
however, were always so good, and pos-
sessed such an amiable temper, as to make
every one your friend. I have heard much
in your praise from the American gentlemen who have been in Brazil, when, you
may be sure, I asked hundreds of ques-

tions about you all. My two dear children
(only two) are well, and grown so much you
would not know them. They speak English, Spanish, and Portuguese fluently, and
are learning French. I find I cannot now
say a word in that language I do not want
them to understand. Give my love (yes
love!) to Mr. Madison, and ask him if he
has entirely forgotten me, and the dear old
times? And when you write to Mr. Jefferson's daughter, Mrs. Randolph, pray remember me particularly to her. She is a
sweet woman, and I have a great regard
for her. The Marquis desires his best
compliments to yourself and Mr. Madison.
And believe me, my dear Mrs. Madison,
your old and affectionate friend,

SALLY D'YRUJO.

GENERAL LAFAYETTE TO MR. MADISON.

PARIS, *Germinal the* 10*th,* 11*th year.*

MY DEAR MADISON, — General Bernadotte is so gloriously introduced by his
own reputation and character, that I shall
only present him to you as my personal
friend. He is of all men the one I should
prefer to see going to America as an ambassador, was he not also the man whom

all true and steady patriots cannot but heartily wish to keep nearer to his own country, where none surpass and few can equal the sincerity and steadiness of his republican civism. Madame Bernadotte accompanies him on this mission, and I hope the amiable consort of the general will meet from our American ladies the reception to which she is so well entitled. She particularly wishes to obtain the friendship of Mrs. Madison, and I have no doubt, from the knowledge of your mutual sentiments, that the intimacy will be soon established between the two families. Mr. Livingstone's correspondence will acquaint you with the political transactions of Europe, and the situation of affairs respecting America. I shall the less expatiate on these points as I am under very painful operations, resulting from an accident, the particulars of which may be given you by General Bernadotte. With heartfelt gratitude, but without surprise, I have heard in how friendly a way you have interested yourself about my affairs.

I hope a long letter from me . . . has reached you. May the affair of Louisiana be settled in a satisfactory manner, so that her passage to the situation of an united and independent commonwealth, as it cannot fail in every chance to be soon the case, be not attended with any disagreement between the two countries to whom I am so patriotically bound. Adieu, my dear sir.

I am most affectionately your old and constant friend,   LAFAYETTE.

Madame Serurier, the wife of another Minister from France, was a great pet and friend of Mrs. Madison. She is represented as being wonderfully beautiful and attractive, and withal the heroine of quite a romantic story. Her parents, Mr. and Mrs. Pageot, then living in New York, were refugees from the island of St. Domingo. Their flight had been attended by many hair-breadth escapes, until reaching the vessel which was to bear them away from their troubles they began to breathe more freely and to consider themselves comparatively safe.

This feeling of confidence, however, was premature ; that night just before sailing, a band of natives who had followed up the fugitives came on board, and discovering the objects of their search were on the point of murdering them, when the cries awakening their daughter, then only a child of seven years, she rushed on deck, clad in the little white gown in which she had been sleeping, and, throwing herself at the feet of the brutal negroes, implored them to spare the lives of her parents. Astonished and superstitious, half believing it was a spirit before them, they paused and gradually dispersed, leaving the ship to make the most of its opportunity to escape. Directly on their arrival, Monsieur Serurier brought her to one of Mrs. Madison's drawing-rooms, where she conceived a most enthusiastic and lasting friendship for her hostess. Twenty years later Monsieur Serurier was again appointed to represent France in Washington, and their friendship was renewed by a long and enjoyable visit to Montpelier.

CHAPTER X.

MANY houses were offered to the President on his return to Washington, and for a year he rented a building called the Octagon, owned by Colonel Taylor, and there it was that the treaty of peace was signed. Afterwards he removed to the northwest corner of Pennsylvania Avenue and Nineteenth Street, to a large house, which had previously been occupied by the Treasury Department.

The White House was repaired only in time for Mr. Monroe. An old citizen says "that the drawing-room of Mrs. Madison in February, 1816, was remembered for years as the most brilliant ever held up to that date in the Executive Mansion. The Justices of the Supreme Court were present in their gowns, at the head of whom was Chief Justice Marshall. The Peace Commissioners to Ghent — Gallatin, Bayard, Clay, and Russell — were in the company.

Mr. Adams alone was absent. The levee was made additionally brilliant by the heroes of the War of 1812, Major-Generals Brown, Gaines, Scott, and Ripley, with their aids, all in full dress uniform, forming an attractive feature. The return of peace had restored the kindest feeling at home and abroad. The Federalists and Democrats of both Houses of Congress, party politicians, citizens, and strangers, were brought together as friends to be thankful for the present, and to look forward with security to the future.

The Diplomatic Corps, too, was well represented in the gorgeousness of court dress, prominent in which was Sir Charles Bagot, special ambassador from our late enemy, Great Britain. It was on this occasion that he made the remark that " Mrs. Madison looked every inch a queen."

Two plain ladies from the West, passing through Washington, determined not to leave without seeing Mrs. Madison; and having but little time were very much puzzled how to accomplish it.

Meeting an old gentleman in the street early next morning, who happened to be a friend of Mrs. Madison's, they timidly ex-

plained their wish, and requested him to
show them the way to the President's
house. Pleased with their simplicity he
took pleasure in conducting them himself,
where he found the family at breakfast.
Mrs. Madison good-naturedly went in to
the parlor to be inspected, and put the old
ladies quite at their ease by her cordial
welcome.

Their astonishment, however, at seeing
so great a personage in a dark gray stuff
dress, with a white apron, and kerchief
pinned across her breast was unbounded,
but so reassuring, that when the time came
for leaving, one of them said : " P'r'aps
you would n't mind if I just kissed you, to
tell my girls about." Mrs. Madison, not
to be outdone by her guests' politeness,
gracefully embraced them both, and after
many expressions of admiration and friend-
liness the delighted old ladies departed.

At a drawing-room held by Mrs. Madison in 1813 " General Harrison was the
subject of a dispute between a lady of
great beauty and high connections and Mr.
Madison. She observed when she went in
that General Harrison had received her
commands to meet her at the reception

this evening. 'But that he cannot do,' said the President, 'because he left Washington this morning, with his horses and attendants, from the door of this house, and must now be some twenty or thirty miles on his way to the West.' 'Still,' replied the lady, laughing, 'he must be here, for I laid my command upon him, and he is too gallant a man to disobey me.' The President rejoined with his manner of gentle but positive assurance, 'We shall soon see whose orders he obeys,' when the door opened and General Harrison appeared with his military attendants in full uniform, and the lady smiled her triumph over the most successful General of that day and the President of the United States."

Until the close of Mr. Madison's troubled administration in 1817, Mrs. Madison continued to dispense her hospitalities in the same hearty, simple manner, having among her guests from time to time many distinguished men, among whom were Thomas Moore, Talleyrand, Chateaubriand, Volney, General Moreau, Joseph and Jerome Bonaparte, Dr. Priestly, the celebrated philosopher and polemical divine, and others.

It had been said by a foreigner that "her table was more like a harvest home supper than the entertainment of a high official." These and similar remarks came to her ears, and she observed with a smile, "that to her, abundance was preferable to elegance ; that circumstances formed customs, and customs formed taste ; and as the profusion so laughed at by foreigners arose from the happy circumstance of the superabundance and prosperity of our country, she did not hesitate to sacrifice the delicacy of European taste for the less elegant, but more liberal, fashion of Virginia."

Washington had so long been the home of Mrs. Madison that it was with much regret she prepared to leave it. Many and dear were her friends, and they united in showing every attention that affection and respect could dictate. The actual departure was delayed for some time by the many entertainments given in honor of the Ex-President and his wife.

From a letter written by a Virginia lady, who was once an inmate of the White House, we take the following extract : —

"My recollections of Mrs. Madison are

of the most agreeable nature, and were formed from a long and intimate acquaintance, beginning in my childhood and ending only with her life. She had a sweet natural dignity of manner, which attracted while it commanded respect ; a proper degree of reserve without stiffness in company with strangers; and a stamp of frankness and sincerity, which, with her intimate friends, became gayety and playfulness of manner. There was, too, a cordial, genial, sunny atmosphere surrounding her which won all hearts — and was one of the secrets of her popularity. She was said to be, during Mr. Madison's administration, the most popular person in the United States, and she certainly had a remarkable memory for names and faces. No person introduced to Mrs. Madison at one of the crowded levees at the White House required a second presentation on meeting her again, but had the gratification of being recognized and addressed by name. Her son, Payne Todd, was a worthless fellow, and his behavior was the great sorrow of her life. Mr. Madison, during his lifetime, bore with him like a father, and paid many of his

debts ; but he was an incorrigible spend-
thrift, and spent his own fortune and his
mother's too, embittering the last years of
her life."

TO MRS. MADISON FROM MRS. LEE.

WASHINGTON, *March* 4, 1817.

MY DEAR FRIEND, — On this day eight
years ago, I wrote from the retirement of
Sully to congratulate you on the joyful
event that placed you in the highest station our country can bestow. I then enjoyed the proudest feelings — that my
friend, the friend of my youth, who never
had forsaken me, should be thus distinguished, and so peculiarly fitted for it.

How much greater cause have I to congratulate you at this period, for having so
filled it as to render yourself more envi-
able this day than your successor, as it is
more difficult to deserve the gratitude and
thanks of the community than their congratulations. You have most decidedly
deserved all of this. Being deprived, by
the sickness of my child, from joining the
multitude to-day in paying my respects
where they are due, I feel the sweetest

consolation in devoting myself to you.
My heart clings to you, my beloved friend,
and has done so for the last fortnight, with
a selfishness that produces the keenest
feelings of regret, and though my domestic
habits, more than inclination, have prevented my taking advantage of your kind
invitations to be more with you, yet I felt
a security and pleasure in being so near
you, and a confidence in your affection,
that constituted my chief pride as a citizen, I assure you. But the period has at
length arrived when we must again part.
You will retire from the tumult and fatigue of public life to your favorite retreat
in Orange County, and will carry with you
principles and manners not to be put off
with the robe of state, having been drawn
from maternal breasts, and nurtured from
the example of those dear, pious parents,
to whom you ever resigned yourself with
such filial obedience and devotion as to
bring their blessings on your head. Talents such as yours were never intended
to remain inactive ; on retiring from public life, you will form a more fortunate arrangement of your time, be able to display
them in the more noble and interesting

walks of life. You will cherish them, my
dear friend, in a more native soil ; they
will constitute the chief felicity of your
dear, venerated husband, and descend in
full perfection to your son. I remember
at this moment, in my last conversation
with my venerable uncle, your father's
friend, he said of you, " She will hold out
to the end ; she was a dutiful daughter,
and never turned her back on an old
friend, and was charitable to the poor."
Will you do me the favor, dear Dolly, —
for it is near my heart that you should, —
take advantage of some leisure moment
to say something for me to your husband.
In the fullness of my gratitude I can express nothing, but shall ever hold in remembrance the highly valued friendship
and confidence he has shown my husband.
I rejoice to hear that you do not leave the
city very soon, and may hope to enjoy
your society, though I presume your engagements are most numerous just now.
I must ask your pardon for thrusting such
an epistle upon you, but it relieves my
heart, and will not, I trust, wound yours ;
it demands no other acknowledgment, at
present, than a cordial reception. It

grows dark, and I want you to have this on this momentous evening.

Believe me most truly yours,

Eliza Lee.

There were many persons who ascribed to Mrs. Madison a degree of influence over the public conduct of her husband far greater than really existed. That her opinions, even upon public affairs, had great weight with her husband is unquestionably true, for he frequently gave his testimony to the solidity of her advice; but there is no evidence that it either originated or materially altered any part of the course he had laid out for himself. Whenever she differed in sentiment from him, she perfectly understood her own position, and that the best way of recommending her views was by entire concession. A word said after the mood had passed would receive great consideration from him; her influence was of that calm, negative order, which often prevents evil consequences from momentary indiscretion.

CHAPTER XI.

MR. MADISON's second term having expired, and his Secretary of State, James Monroe, being installed in the Presidency, he gladly retired to his dearly-loved Montpelier, where with a few congenial friends around him, he could still give a large proportion of his time to his favorite studies. He was a silent, grave man, whose nature was relieved by a vein of quaint, quiet humor, which, in his moments of relaxation, gave an inexpressible charm to his presence. A statesman of an unusually sound mind and great research, his diplomatic correspondence was remarkable for its clearness and precision ; the language, well-chosen and to the point, showed a cool, clear judgment, which caused him to be referred to in matters of importance, even before and after his many years of public life.

He combined with a free and manly expression of his opinions an observance of parliamentary courtesy, worthy of the dignity of his character, and of the gravity and importance of the question at issue. His style of dress was never altered : plain black cloth coat and knee - breeches with buckles, the hair powdered and worn in a queue behind ; the daily task of dressing it devolved upon his wife, who would not think his body-servant capable of doing it justice.   He was a decided contrast to Mrs. Madison, who was still blooming, and showed little sign of the forty five years she was entitled to.   Always handsomely. and becomingly dressed, her matronly figure had not yet outgrown the grace and dignity so much admired.

He shared with General Washington and Mr. Jefferson a great predilection for agricultural pursuits, and Montpelier, his father's residence, had always been his home during the few months in summer that he was enabled to throw off partially the cares of official life.   He devoted himself with great earnestness, as well as a keen relish, to the tranquil and tranquilizing pursuits of the country, identifying himself with all its familiar and home-bred interests, and embarking with zeal in every plan for the improvement of agriculture, its processes, and its implements. A few extracts from the almost daily correspondence between him and Mr. Jefferson, at the time of one of his congressional vacations, will show the primitive tastes of these two statesmen, which with Washington made them the true representatives of the great agricultural classes and interests of America.

In his first letter from Virginia he says : "Our fields continue to anticipate a luxuriant harvest. The greatest danger is apprehended from too rapid a vegetation, under the present warm weather. . . . Will you be so good, in case an opportunity should offer, to inquire of Dr. Logan as to the ploughs he was to have made and sent to Mrs. House's for me." In a letter a few weeks later, he speaks with the anxiety and minuteness of a practical farmer, of the unfavorable change which the intervening period had made in the prospects of the crops.

"Our fine prospects in the wheat-field have been severely injured by the weather for some time past. The wheat had gotten safe into the head, and with tolerable weather would have ripened into a most exuberant harvest. . . . Should the weather be ever so favorable henceforward, a considerable proportion will be lost."

Mr. Jefferson found time, in the midst of his absorbing duties as Secretary of State, to execute the commission of his friend, and to indulge his yearnings for the country life from which he was so reluctantly parted. In a letter on the 9th of June, 1793, he says to Mr. Madison: "Your ploughs shall be duly attended to. Have you taken notice of Tull's horse-shoeing plough? I am persuaded that it is good where you wish your work to be very exact, and our great plough, where a less degree of exactness is required, leaves us nothing to wish for from other countries as to ploughs, under our circumstances. I have not yet received my (Scotch) threshing-machine. I fear the late long and heavy rains have extended to 'us, and affected our wheat."

These allusions to rural life, and its interests and occupations, recur perpetually in all the letters of the two friends, in the midst of the gravest discussions on the country's welfare, and exhibits, besides, another pleasing feature in Mr. Madison's character as a country gentleman. He gave himself up with a free and congenial spirit to the duties of hospitality and the calls of social intercourse and friendship. He goes to pay promised visits to two friends in the neighboring county of Albemarle, Colonel Monroe and Colonel Wilson Cary Nicholas; and on his return writes to Mr. Jefferson : "I find the house full of particular friends, who will stay some weeks, receiving and returning visits, from which I cannot decently exclude myself, even for my dear library."

We are tempted to pursue still further the unreserved correspondence of these two congenial friends; in one letter, where Mr. Jefferson feels so anxious to return to Monticello, that he is seriously tempted to resign the portfolio of State ; and in another, where he writes to urge Mr. Madison to purchase a farm in the immediate vicinity of his own home, " a nice little place," he adds, " which purchase would add so much to my happiness."

Enough has been said, however, to show the spirit with which Mr. Madison turned his back upon Washington, and the cares

of office, devoting himself to his favorite
pursuits, reading and farming, for the remaining years of his life.   Mrs. Madison,
too, was devoted to Montpelier, and led a
busy life among her household of guests,
and the many interests of gardens and
poor people.   Mr. Madison senior, and his
eldest son Ambrose, had both passed away,
leaving the property, which comprised
2,500 acres, to James, who enlarged the
house to make room for friends, without
interfering at all with his mother's household.   She lived to the age of ninety-eight
years, retaining the use of all the original
part of the old homestead, and keeping up
the old-fashioned hours ; waited upon by
servants who had grown old in her service.
One old negro at ninety, with a halo of
gray hair about his head, refused to allow
any one to take his place behind his mistress's chair, though sleep sometimes made
him totter in a most alarming manner.

General Lafayette, when he visited Montpelier in his last journey to this country in
1825, enjoyed going about with Mrs. Madison to all the different cabins occupied
by the negroes, one of whom, Granny
Milly, a hundred and four years old, lived

with her daughter and granddaughters, the youngest seventy years of age, all retired from their labors. These became great friends of his, and he would stroll down to the " Walnut Grove " for a little chat, coming back with a fresh egg, or a nosegay presented by the old people.

The house of Montpelier lay on a very pretty slope of land, surrounded by the Blue Ridge Mountains, which extended as far as the eye could reach, with little vistas of country roads winding in and out; roads eagerly scanned with a telescope, which was part of the portico furniture, when carriages were almost daily seen, bringing friends, or even strangers, who wished to pay their respects to the host and hostess. Tourists on the road to the Virginia Springs were told at Orange Court House that they were only five miles from Ex-President Madison's, and though hesitating to intrude upon his privacy, they most of them found their way to the hospitable mansion, and were reassured by the cordiality of their reception.

A contemporary writer, describing Montpelier, says : "There are few houses in Virginia that gave a larger welcome, or made

it more agreeable, than that over which
' Queen Dolly,' the most gracious and beloved of all our female sovereigns, reigned,
and wielding as skillfully the domestic, as
she had done worthily and popularly the
public, sceptre; everything that came beneath her immediate and personal sway,
the care and entertainment of visitors, the
government of servants, the whole policy
of the interior, was admirably managed
with equal grace and efficacy."

The house had a very large, wide portico in front, supported by pillars, where
Mr. Madison exercised in stormy weather,
walking his allotted number of miles.   In
the centre of the gravel walk to the first
gate, a large tin cup was imbedded to show
the amount of rain fallen, which was carefully measured and brought to him, after a
shower, and on the right hand a path bor-
dered with silver pine led to a little building in the form of a temple, surmounted
by a statue of Liberty, and intended for his
study ; from this, groups of trees — silver
poplar and weeping willow — concealed the
numerous out-buildings so essential to a
southern country - house.   Back of the
house was another large portico, opening

on an extensive lawn, bounded by a ha-ha
hedge, and with two large tulip-trees in the
centre, so exactly alike that Mr. Madison
named them "the twins;" they were still
standing a few years ago in a field, surrounded by a quantity of tiger-lilies, the
product of seed sent from France by General Lafayette. Our much-abused thistle,
too, was first propagated in that region by
a package of seeds from the same source,
marked "very rare."

At some distance from the house was a
garden laid out in the form of a large
horse-shoe, and kept in perfect order by a
French gardener, named Beazée. This
Beazée and his wife came to Virginia at
the time of the French Revolution, and
made themselves very popular with the
slaves, taking the trouble to teach some of
the more enlightened ones to speak French,
much to the amusement of their mistress,
who laughed very heartily over the jargon.
The wife was a good woman, with a very
voluble tongue, and who delighted to please
"Madame" in any way. She exercised
her ingenuity in manufacturing a very
ugly shade hat, which Mrs. Madison called
her "Beazée bonnet," and wore during
her morning rambles about the place.

Fruits of all kinds, including figs, flowers, and plants, many of them rare and delicate, sent by admiring friends, made the grounds most attractive to guests. Roses and white jessamine entwined the pillars of the south portico, creeping up to the terraces and making the summer air rich with perfume, as it stole in through the long drawing-room windows. The "old lady," as she was called, had her own separate garden, laid out in the most prim, old-fashioned manner by her own gardener. No innovation of any kind was allowed in her domain. She was a woman of strong mind and good education, active and bright up to the last days of her life, taking a great interest and pride in the friends visiting her son and daughter, who were brought to see her and her quaint surroundings at two o'clock, the hour set apart for receiving. At this hour she was to be found seated upon a couch in the centre of a large room, with a table by her side, containing her Bible and prayer-book, which, with her knitting, divided her time ; the innumerable gloves and stockings made by her, with the names knitted in, were presented to those whom she fancied among the guests. The long hall, with its highly polished floor, connecting the old wing with the main part of the house, was hung with pictures, and led into the large dining-room in which were many portraits. Napoleon in his ermine robes, Louis the Fourteenth, Confucius, several members of the family, and faithful slaves, together with a water-color painting of Mr. Jefferson by his enthusiastic admirer Kosciusko, — these with the many medallions and other testimonials of respect and admiration from crowned heads as well as friends, covered the walls, while the large, polished mahogany table and sideboard were bright with silver, the accumulation of three families. Out of this opened Mr. Madison's sitting-room, furnished with chairs and bed of iron, brought by Mr. Monroe from the dismantled palace of the Tuileries ; the last with very high posts, and a heavy canopy of crimson damask.

Here, with his own desk and papers around him, he spent much time, and towards the latter years of his life, when rheumatism crippled his fingers so that he could not manage the knife, he dined at a small table, placed sufficiently near

the door of the dining-room to permit conversation with his guests. Another door
opened into a room filled with statuary,
called the " clock-room," out of respect to
an old-fashioned English clock, which regu-
lated the household for many years. There
were some fifty statues and busts, including
those of Washington, Jefferson and the
elder Adams, with a very excellent profile
of himself in marble by Carricci, who afterwards lost his life in prison from having invented the infernal machine. The
drawing-room was carpeted with Persian
rugs, the walls were quite covered with
mirrors and pictures, six of which last
were by Stuart, and the framed Declaration of Independence; while many pretty
bits of furniture and china made the
room look cheerful and homelike, as one
glanced through the glass doors leading
in from the lawn. From the front hall the
carved oaken staircase led up-stairs to the
bedrooms and the library, the latter not
only lined with book-cases, but the centre
so filled with them that there was only
just room enough to pass among them.
Books and pamphlets were piled up everywhere, on every available chair and table,

accumulated by Mr. Madison and his father, who shared the same literary tastes.
Added to their own collection was the
valuable library of Lord Dunmore, bought
by the elder Madison, and left at his son's
death to the University of Virginia.

With this pleasant home, full of friends
and waited upon by devoted slaves, the
days passed quickly enough; only once
did Mr. and Mrs. Madison leave Montpelier for any distance, and that was to go
to Richmond, where he attended the convention for revising the Constitution of
Virginia. Here they were very pleasantly
entertained; the people, famed for their
hospitality, were delighted to welcome the
Ex-President and his wife, who, after a few
weeks of gayety, were glad to return home
to their more quiet country life.

Mrs. Madison had been very much drawn
to the Episcopal Church before leaving
Washington, and though five miles of bad
road intervened between her home and the
nearest church at Orange Court House,
both Mr. Madison and herself, with such
guests as were of the same mind, took the
long drive every fair Sunday until failing

health kept him at home and her to keep him company.

One of the great occasions for bringing the neighbors together from far and near were the camp-meetings, looked forward to with great pleasure and participated in by old and young of all denominations. Barbecues, too, were at the height of their popularity. At these feasts the woods were alive with carriages, horses, servants, and children ; farmers exchanged ideas about crops and politics, while a long table was spread under the forest oaks, and heaped with good things of every kind. Animals were roasted whole, the punch-bowl passed from lip to lip accompanied by an appetite whetted by the invigorating mountain air, "and the pleasure of clasping hands with neighbors seen only at meeting time." The woods rang with merriment. If not too late, fiddles were produced by some of the negroes, and a dance ended the day, the guests departing reluctantly and according to the number of miles before them, while the negroes, after a feast off the remains of the repast, made the night melodious with their wild, sweet songs·

TO MR. EDWARD COLES.

MONTPELIER, *September* 3, 1819.

I have received, my dear sir, your agreeable letter, which lingered a long time on
the way.

We congratulate you much on the various successes of your western career, and
the first thing that strikes us is the rapid-
ity of your promotions. Bounding over
the preliminary sailorship, the first step
on the deck of your bark — pardon me, of
the noble structure the Ark — makes you
a pilot; the name of pilot is scarcely pronounced before you are a captain ; and in
less than the twinkling of an eye the captain starts up a commodore. On the land
a scene opens out before us in which you,
too, figure. We see you at once a plough-
man, a rail-splitter, a fence-builder, a corn-
planter, and a hay-maker. To all these
rural functions, which leave but a single
defect in your title of husband-(man), you
add the facilities of a town life. And to
cap the whole you enjoy the official dignity
of "Register of the Land Office" in the
important Territory of Illinois. We repeat
our congratulations on all these honors

and employments, and wish that the emoluments may equal them.

You are well off, for this year at least, when you can expect bread from corn planted in July. Here, famine threatens us in the midst of fields planted in April. So severe a drought is not remembered. On some farms, and among them my two small ones near home, there has been no rain at all, or none to produce any sensible effect. It has been, I hear, particularly hard upon the tobacco crop in Virginia, and will make a bad year.

You are pursuing, I observe, the true course with your negroes in order to make their freedom a fair experiment for their happiness. With the habits of the slave and without the instruction, property, or employments of a freeman, the blacks, instead of deriving advantage from the partial benevolence of their masters, furnish arguments against the general efforts in their behalf. I wish your philanthropy could complete its object by changing their color as well as their legal condition. Without this they seem destined to a privation of that moral rank and those social blessings which give to freedom more than half its value. Mrs. Madison as well as myself is much gratified by your promise to devote the next winter to your native haunts. We sincerely hope your arrangements will give us an ample share of your time. We will then take the case of your bachelorship into serious and full consideration. Mrs. Madison is well disposed to give all her aid in getting that old thorn out of your side, and putting a young rib in its place. She very justly remarks, however, that with your own exertions hers will not be wanted, and without them not deserved.

Accept our joint wishes for your health and every other happiness.

JAMES MADISON.

Payne Todd came home from Europe, after several years of traveling which made large inroads into his fortune, and bought an estate in Virginia. Much of his time, however, was spent in Philadelphia and Washington, or in wandering about, to his mother's sorrow, who had been very anxious to have him marry and settle down to a profession.

TO PAYNE TODD, ESQ.

MONTPELIER, *April* 9, 1823.

I am impatient to hear from you, my dearest Payne, and had I known where to direct I should have written you before this : not that there is anything particular to communicate, but for the pleasure of repeating how much I love you, and to hear of your happiness.

Your father received the journal of "Las Casas," with your name in it, from Philadelphia, which is an indication that you are there, and I write accordingly. We returned yesterday from Monticello, after passing three days with Mr. Jefferson and one with Judge Nelson.

Ellen and Virginia were indisposed, but all the others, with Mr. Jefferson, are well ; they hoped to have seen you with us. I inclose a letter your father received from General Taylor, as, perhaps, you might draw on him without knowing his payment was intended to be made you so soon. Let me know when you propose leaving Philadelphia and your route, that I may send you some commissions. Adieu, my dear boy   Your father joins me in affectionate wishes for you.   Your

MOTHER.

TO PAYNE TODD, ESQ.

MONTPELIER, *December* 2, 1824.

I have received yours, my dearest Payne, of the 23d and 24th of November, and was impatient to answer them yesterday, — the day of their reaching me, — but owing to the winter arrangement for the mail, no post leaves this until to-morrow morning. Mr. Clay inquired affectionately after you; he with two members of Congress have been passing several days with us.   Every one inquires after you; but, my dear son, it seems to be the wonder of them all that you should stay away from us for so long a time! and now I am ashamed to tell, when asked, how long my only child has been absent from the home of his mother. Your father and I entreat you to come to us; to arrange your business with those concerned, so that you may return to them when necessary, and let us see you here as soon as possible with your interest and convenience.   Your father thinks as I do, that it would be best for your reputation and happiness, as well as ours, that you should consult your parents on subjects of deep account to you, and that you would find it so on returning to Philadelphia at the appointed time, which shall be whenever you wish it. I have said in my late letters, as well as this, all that I thought sufficient to influence you. I must now put my trust in God alone ! . . .

I can add no news that is likely to interest you, except about poor Judge Todd, who is very ill ; and that Ellen Randolph is to be married to Mr. Coolidge. We should rejoice in any occurrence that would bring you speedily to our arms, who love you with inexpressible tenderness and constancy. Your own   MOTHER.

TO MRS. MADISON FROM MRS. PHŒBE
MORRIS.

WASHINGTON, *January* 19, 1824.

MY DEAREST MRS. MADISON, — I have been in Washington about a fortnight, where everything reminds me of you ; but alas ! sometimes painfully, for so many scenes of joy and sorrow have passed since the happy period of my early youth, which was rendered more joyous by your protect-

ing care. We are very comfortably established together at the "six buildings." I
often think of you and my dear Mr. Madison alone at Montpelier, for you have told
me that there is not so much visiting in
winter. I know all your motions and ways
so well, that at any hour of the day I can
represent to myself what you are doing.
What do you think of the probability of
having the Marquis de Lafayette for a
visit, for surely Montpelier will be the first
place to fly to, when he comes to the
United States. The Secretary of the
Navy says he shall have one of the finest
and best manned vessels in the service to
convey him hither, if Mitchell's resolution
is carried, and he wishes to come, which
does not appear as yet quite decided.

Mrs. Monroe is really going to have a
drawing-room on Wednesday. You have
no doubt seen the description of Mrs.
Hays's personal elegance of deportment
and costume in the papers. We all attended Mrs. Adams's reception on the 8th,
and it was really a very brilliant party,
and admirably well arranged. The ladies
climbed the chairs and benches to see General Jackson, and Mrs. Adams very grace-

fully took his arm, and walked through the apartments with him, which gratified the general curiosity.

It is said there were fourteen hundred cards issued, and about eight hundred supposed to be present.

I would like to hear something of Miss Willis ; whenever I feel a little romantic, and think of some pure and innocent being, sheltered from the storms of life, and lovely in the bosom of retreat, my imagination turns to that sweet and sympathetic girl. I beg you will remember me to her affectionately, my dearest friend, also to her excellent mother. How is your mother, Mrs. Madison ? I hope she is as bright and active as ever : give my love and respectful admiration to her. Adieu, my dearest and best friend ; believe me, as ever,   Your own affectionate

PHŒBE MORRIS.

TO MRS. ANDREW STEVENSON.

MONTPELIER, —— 1826.

I have received by post just now, my ever dear cousin, your welcome letter, and cannot express my anxiety to embrace you once more ; but a spell rests upon me, and

withholds me from those I love most in
this world; not a mile can I go from
home; and in no way can I account for it,
but that my husband is fixed here, and
hates to have me leave him. This is the
third winter in which he has been engaged
in the arrangement of papers, and the business seems to accumulate as he proceeds,
so that it might outlast my patience, and
yet I cannot press him to forsake a duty
so important, or find it in my heart to
leave him during its fulfillment. We very
often speak of you, and the many causes
of our admiration for you, concluding, by
assuring one another, that if we could leave
home this winter, it should be only to visit
you and Mr. Stevenson. Allow us, then,
my dear, to retain the privilege you so
kindly give us, of our rooms, where you
shall some day see us.

This fall I had the pleasure of receiving
a visit from Mrs. Randolph, her sister, and
Ellen; they told me you had been indisposed, and from your silence, I feared you
had not recovered. I receive letters every
week from my sister Anna; she is in a
round of pleasant society, and though devoted as ever to her children, takes time

to enjoy a good dance. Mrs. Brown, whom you may remember, has rented a house near her, gives a great many handsome parties. Mrs. Crawford, Mrs. Adams, and many others keep up the fashion of dissipation. Our love, dear cousin, to you and yours, hoping to see you ere long.

Affectionately yours,

DOLLY MADISON.

Much as she graced her public station, Mrs. Madison has not been less admirable in domestic life. Neighborly and companionable among her country friends, as if she had never lived in a city ; delighting in the society of young people, and promoting their pleasure by her participation and enjoyment of it ; she still proved herself a most affectionate and devoted wife during the years of suffering before Mr. Madison's death. Without neglecting the duties of a kind hostess, a faithful friend and relative, she soothed, occupied, and amused the tiresome hours of his long confinement.

Never, in the midst of a drawing-room, surrounded on all sides by everything that was brilliant and courtly, — the centre of attraction, the object of admiration, — never was she so interesting, so attractive, as in her loving attendance on her venerable mother - in - law, who said, "Dolly is my mother now, and cares most tenderly for all my wants," and later on, in filling the same office to her husband in his declining years.

Monticello was about thirty miles from Montpelier, and in the estimate of a Virginian, Mr. Jefferson and Mr. Madison were neighbors, and visited frequently, over roads so bad that outriders were brought into requisition at times to hold up the coach.

TO ANNA.

MONTPELIER, *July* 5, 1820.

I have just received yours, dearest Anna, and rejoice that you are well and have your friends about you. Yesterday we had ninety persons to dine with us at one table, — put up on the lawn, under a thick arbor. The dinner was profuse and good, and the company very orderly. Many of them were old acquaintance of yours, and among them the two Barbours.

We had no ladies except mother Madison, Mrs. Macon, and Nelly Willis ; the day was cool and pleasant; half a dozen only stayed all night with us, and they are now about to depart. Colonel Monroe's letter this morning announces the advent of the French Minister, and we shall expect him this evening, or perhaps sooner. I am less worried here with an hundred visitors than with twenty-five in Washington, — this summer especially. I wish, dearest, you had just such a country home as this. I truly believe it is the happiest and most true life, and would be so good for you and the dear children.

Always your devoted sister,
DOLLY P. MADISON.

Her nieces and nephews, children of the favorite sister, Anna, were a great delight and pleasure to Mrs. Madison, and she kept up a constant correspondence with them, particularly with Mary, and Dolly her namesake, from their babyhood.

TO HER NIECE, MARY CUTTS.

MONTPELIER, *July* 30, 1826.

Your letter, my dearest niece, with the one before it, came quite safely, for which I return many thanks and kisses. I rejoice too, dear Dolly, to see how well you write and express yourself, and am as proud of all your acquirements as if you were my own daughter. I trust you will yet be with me this summer, when I shall see your improvement in person also, and enjoy the sweet assurance of your affection. Mary Lee and her husband have been indisposed, but are better. They say often they hope you will come with your dear mother, as do all your relatives and friends in this quarter. The old lady, — even the negroes, young and old, want to see you, dear.

We had old Mr. Patterson and his son Edward from Baltimore to stay with us several days, and they tell me that Madame Bonaparte is still in France, and her son gone to Rome to visit his father. Mr. Monroe left us yesterday, disappointed in his views of raising money from his land. Mr. B. continued on his way to the Springs, and I was disappointed at not sending a packet to you, inclosing the flounce which I wanted you to wear, worked by me long ago.

I received by the last post a letter from your cousin Payne, at New York; he

writes in fine health and spirits, and says
he will be detained only a few weeks
longer in that city. I sincerely hope to
see him soon, though it is impossible for
him to prefer Virginia to the North. If I
were in Washington with you I know I
could not conform to the formal rules of
visiting they now have, but would disgrace
myself by rushing about among my friends
at all hours. Here I find it most agreeable
to stay at home, everything around me is
so beautiful. Our garden promises grapes
and figs in abundance, but I shall not enjoy them unless your mamma comes, and
brings you to help us with them ; tell the
boys they must come too. Alas ! poor Walter, away at sea ! I can scarcely trust myself to think of him, — his image fills my
eyes with tears.

Adieu, and believe me always your tender mother and aunt,

DOLLY P. MADISON.

P. S.   We are very old-fashioned here.
Can you send me a paper pattern of the
present sleeve, and describe the width of
dress and waist ; also how turbans are
pinned up, bonnets worn, as well as how
to behave in the fashion ?

TO DOLLY.

MONTPELIER, *March* 10, 1830.

I am now seated, pen in hand, my sweet niece, to write you, though not in the humor for the success I desire in producing an amusing letter such as mine *should* be in answer to yours.

Imagine, if you can, a greater trial to the patience of us farmers than the destruction of a radiant patch of green peas by frost! It came last night on the skirts of a storm; and while I was lamenting that our dear midshipman, Walter, should ever be exposed to such winds, my young adventurers at home were completely wrecked off their moorings! But away with complaints, other patches equally radiant will arise, and I will mourn no longer over a mess of peas or pottage, but would rather meet you somewhere, or hear about your last party. I had, indeed, my *"quantum sufficit"* of gayety in Richmond, but what I enjoyed most was the quiet but thorough hospitality of the inhabitants among whom I should like to spend my winters. Washington, if my old friends were still there, would no doubt be my preference; but I confess I do not admire contention in any form, either political or civil. In my quiet retreat I like to hear of what is going on, and therefore hope, my dear, you will not be timid in telling me, though your statements shall be seen by no one else. I wish that circumstances would have permitted you to have accepted Mr. V. B.'s invitation, but I cannot doubt you had a good reason for declining. By the bye, do you ever get hold of a clever novel, new or old, that you could send me? I bought Cooper's last, but did not care for it, because the story was so full of horrors.

Adieu, my dearest Dolly, think of me as your own friend as well as aunt, and write as often as you can to

Yours affectionately,

DOLLY P. MADISON.

TO DOLLY.

MONTPELIER, *November*, 1830.

DEAREST NIECE, — I have been so much engaged in the book you kindly sent by the last post, that I have scarcely left myself time to thank you for it by this. I will, however, take an early opportunity to show my gratitude by a longer letter.

If you can send me the " Romance of History " I will be very glad, and will make proper dispatch in the perusal of it. Governor Barbour is here and will stay some time. Philippa does not expect to see Washington again for some time, and regrets it much. Her father is now a judge and she a recluse. I find you have no idea yet of the improvement love can make, or you would not surmise that another must have had to do the courting for John. After he became acquainted with S. Carter, his tongue twanged as if sent from a bow! Last winter when I witnessed his attentions to her, and heard him talk and laugh like Ganymede, I knew it was Cupid's act, by the color. She is a sweet girl and I hope you will see her before long, you and my dear Mary.

Ever your affectionate aunt,

DOLLY P. MADISON.

TO MARY.

MONTPELIER, *January* 5, 1831.

DEAREST MARY, — Yours, ending on the 2d of January, came to relieve my oppressed heart with the tidings of your beloved mother's recovery from that extreme illness, under which I knew or feared she was laboring.

I had. written a week ago this day to Dolly and one to you, inclosed to your father, which could hardly have reached you, or you would have yielded to my pleadings for that single line by every post which would tell me your mamma is better and has a prospect of regaining her health. To secure this, my dearest girls, you must help her in every way you can, keep her room quiet, and herself free from the slightest agitation or uneasiness. The nervousness of which Dr. Sim speaks must be attended to with all your delicacy of thought and conduct ; her sufferings have caused it, and now, no one should approach her who is not sensible of the importance of smiles and comfort to one who has been so near the grave. May Heaven sustain and support her for many years to come to bless you with her protecting love.

I inclose " The Oxonians," which I could not read, while my heart was oppressed by fears for you all. We are well and send love.   Your own aunt,

DOLLY P. MADISON.

TO MARY.

MY DEAREST MARY, — I hasten to answer your nice letter in order to obtain
your forgiveness about the mislaid letter ;
I fear Beckey may have used it to kindle
the fire she was so anxious about for her
master, and as far as I can discover col-
lected everything in the way of paper on
my table this morning. It was so short
I hope you can recollect enough of it to
write it again for your amiable correspondent, to whom give my assurance of
love. I am so grieved that your mamma
is not well, but trust it proceeds from
fatigue. Do persuade her to go to see
Mrs. B., and not to worry about household
cares. I hope the alarm of "insurrections"
is over in the city, though every one should
be on guard after this. I am quiet, hearing little about it, and quite helpless if
in danger. Tell Mr. Trist I send him a
few leaves, if not the whole flower, of his
dear lady (Cape Jessamine), who is now
blooming, when all her contemporaries
have changed color and are passing away,
emblematic of her good disposition and

heart, whose fragrance will last until the end.

Your Uncle Madison still wears the bead ring you placed on his finger, and I see him look at it every now and then without saying anything.

My eyes are troubling me, still I write on a great deal of nonsense. To-morrow I expect a large party from Richmond and the lower country to stay with us. I feel very grateful to all those ladies who are so kind to your mother while she is ailing, and could love the blackest Indian who was good to her; indeed, it seems to me I would like to bribe the whole world to make her well. Payne is on the wing again with three gentlemen in his train.

Adieu, dearest niece. Ever yours,

DOLLY MADISON.

TO MARY.

MONTPELIER, *December*, 1831.

MY OWN DEAR NIECE, — I have been the most disconsolate of persons these three or four days, and all because of a violent toothache. The book you mention I will keep unless you say no, while I read the second volume, and send them both to

you by Walter, who is summoned to Philadelphia on the first Monday in January,
and will stop in Washington to see you.

In my last I informed you that Walter
and Payne had been detained abroad by
bad weather, but now they are safe and
sound with us, and we have played chess
and talked together all this time without
the appearance of ennui. Thank my dear
Dolly for her kind letter ; and I rejoice
in her recovery, which is due in a great
measure to the judicious nursing of a good
mother.

I hope you will soon be going to parties,
and give me a detailed account of what is
going forward amongst the various charac-
ters in Washington.

I have so long been confined by the side
of my dear sick husband, never seeing or
hearing outside of his room, that I make a
dull correspondent.

Your uncle is better now than he was
three days ago, and I trust will continue to
mend, but his poor hands are still sore,
and so swollen as to be almost useless, and
so I lend him mine. The music-box is
playing beside me, and seems well adapted
to solitude, as I look out at our mountains,

white with snow, and the winter's wind
sounding loud and cold.   I hope you will
take more than usual care of yourself
this weather, and wish I could cover you
with furs ; but ah ! if I dare indulge in
wishes —

Good night, my love.   Your fond aunt,
DOLLY MADISON.

TO HER SISTER ANNA.

MONTPELIER, *August* 2, 1832.

BELOVED SISTER ANNA, — Mrs. Mason
has just written to me to say you are a
little better, and those dear daughters of
yours, Mary and Dolly, whom I shall ever
feel are my own children, have often con-
soled me by their letters since you were
unable to write.   Your husband and boys
too have written frequently, — all in that
affectionate feeling towards you which
manifested their deep love ; and although
my heart is sad within me, because I cannot see or assist you in your long and painful sickness, yet am I very thankful to the
Almighty for his favors in bestowing such
devoted friends as have surrounded your
pillow.

My dear husband is recovering, I hope,

slowly, though still confined to his bed. He speaks of you to me every day with all the partiality and love of a tender brother, and ardently hopes that we may be long spared to each other.

Mrs. Clay and her husband did not call to see me as we expected. They understood that General Jackson was at Montpelier and passed on to Governor Barbour's. The next day Mr. Clay came for a few hours, but did not meet the President here. I regretted much not seeing Mrs. Clay, as she would have talked to me of you.

Do, dear sister, strive to get well and strong for my sake and your children's; what should we do without you! As soon as my eyes are well I will write to dear Mrs. B. In the mean time offer her my love and thanks for all her goodness to you.

Adieu, my dear, ever and always,

Your loving sister,

DOLLY P. MADISON.

Two days after this letter Mrs. Madison received the news of her sister's death, and though in a measure prepared for it, the blow seemed to fall so heavily upon her that she aged very much in a week;

her friends said that for the first time she lost her bright cheerfulness, and from that day until the second shock came upon her of Mr. Madison's death, everything seemed to be an effort.

MONTPELIER, *August* 5, 1832.

DEAR BROTHER, — The heart of your miserable sister mourns with you and for your dear children.

Come to us as soon as you can, and bring them all with you ; I am as deeply interested in them as if they were my own. Where are her remains ? I will my-self write my gratitude to the kind friends who were privileged to do what I could not for my lamented sister.

Mr. Madison partakes in our sorrows, and in my wish to see you all here.   Show this to Dolly and Mary, please, as I can-not write to them at this moment.   Yours came yesterday.

Affectionately your sister,
DOLLY P. MADISON.

TO MARY.

MONTPELIER, *August* 1, 1833.

May your fortune, dearest Mary, be even

better than the sybil's predictions. There is one secret, however, she did not tell you, and that is the power we all have in forming our own destinies.

We must press on that intricate path leading to perfection and happiness, by doing all that is good and noble, before we can be taken under the silver wing of our rewarding angel ; this I feel sure you will aim at, and succeed beyond doubt. It will not be necessary, dear child, to recapitulate all the virtues important to render us worthy and deserving of good fortune, because you know them well.

I received your last letter just a week after the date on the inside, though the envelope was marked for the 26th.

I hope the book I sent has been received, and that ere this you are ready to go on your visit to Cousin William. Present me affectionately to him and the girls ; I should delight in seeing them all. Your Uncle Madison mends in his health, but has many relapses. We have had more company this summer than I can enumerate, and though I enjoy it, my health has not been so good as usual ; this morning I was not able to breakfast with my eight

guests, but went for a drive with my dear
husband and shall join them at dinner.

Your affectionate aunt,

DOLLY P. MADISON.

TO DOLLY.

MONTPELIER, *September* 9, 1833.

It has seemed to me, my dearest Dolly,
that I should never be able to write you a
letter on account of a stream of people
coming and going, until I fear I am quite
nervous.   There is not much of interest to
tell you.   Our neighborhood is as you left
it ; many lowlanders have been among us,
and Mrs. Needham Washington is now
with Mrs. Cole.

Do you know, my dear, that I was as
glad to get a letter from you yesterday as
I was to receive a present of a pair of
the celebrated English Holkim calves, sent
me by Mr. Patterson, of Baltimore.   Your
Uncle Madison is better, and rides out
every day, three or four miles, and these
are the only excursions I have taken since
you left us.   Mr. Longacre was here for
some days to take your uncle's likeness
for his gallery, and I think succeeded very
well.

I do not know if I wrote you that Mr.
Livingstone sent me a fine bust of himself
as a remembrance, before sailing, and I
prize it very much. A young artist named
Chapman is coming to take your uncle's
portrait; we also expect Mr. and Mrs.
Rives, Mr. and Mrs. Stevenson, and many
others, on their way from the White Sulphur Springs. Payne is at home and improving his knowledge of geology.

Ever your own aunt,

DOLLY P. MADISON.

MONTPELIER, *December* 2, 1834.

There has been a spell upon my fingers
for a long time, dearest niece, and even
now there rests one on my eyes ; still I
would commune with you, whom I love so
much, and tell you that your letters are all
received, and my spirits rising as I peruse
them, because my hopes are renewed for
dear Walter in your amiable efforts to em-
bark him again on the waves of fortune.
I rejoice at the pleasant visit you made to
Kalorama with dear Dolché. I was anxious to write and tell you of our visit from
Miss Martineau, and how much we en-

joyed her enlightened conversation and unassuming manners. We also liked her lively little friend, Miss Jeffries. Ah me! my eyes are even now so troublesome that I must hasten to say as much as I can in a short space of time, hoping to do more when they are better.

I have no idea of the new dance you speak of, or its motions, but approve of your declining to learn it, if disapproved of by society. Our sex are ever losers, when they stem the torrent of public opinion. Baron K.'s parties must be piquant and agreeable, but if Sir Charles Vaughn leaves what will you all do?

Your uncle is still about the same, but I hope as the season advances he will gain strength again. With much love to all the dear ones,   Always your own aunt,

DOLLY P. MADISON.

TO PAYNE TODD.

MONTPELIER, *July* 20, 1834.

Yours, dearest, promising to write me again, came safely, and I was glad to hear mine, with the inclosure, had reached you. You did not tell me whether you had been successful in your collections. If not, you will want supplies proportioned to your detention ; I am anxious that you should have them, and you know the little I have in my power is at your command, though but "a drop in the bucket." You will tell me when you intend to return, that I may have the pleasure of expecting you.

Messrs. Patton and Rives dined with us on the 12th ; they inquired for you, and said they had hoped to see you at the party as a " Jackson man." General Madison came with them, looking well and happy. Mr. Madison is better, though very ill a few days since, and I now hope he will soon be well enough for me to leave him on an expedition to the Court House. It would be quite an event for me to go there, five miles from home. Our last tobacco was a failure ; it sold at seven when seventeen was expected ; so it goes with planters. Dolly and Mary wrote me yesterday that you were very popular in Washington, and I should like to be with you to witness it — the respect and love shown to my son would be the highest gratification the world could bestow upon me. I think to inclose this to my brother to deliver, in case of your having left, to

keep it for you, or return when you are
at home, as I shall inclose. . . . We have
seen but few strangers since you left home.
Mr. Burney, of Baltimore, called on his way
to the Springs, and Mr. Randall, of Philadelphia, with his daughters and niece. He
said, by the way, that he had caught a
glimpse of you at the station, but lost sight
of you again, as he was busy with his baggage.

I suppose you saw Madame Serurier before she went on her travels. If you can
see Mrs. Lear, tell her she must come
from the Springs to visit me. And now
adieu, my dear son ; may Heaven preserve and protect you, prays

Your mother,   DOLLY P. MADISON.

TO DOLLY.

MONTPELIER, *May* 11, 1835.

DEAREST DOLLY, — Payne met a friend
(Mr. H.) of yours yesterday at Orange
Court House, and brought him home to
dinner, with his two cousins. We were
much pleased with his society, as well as
the account he gave of you and Mary. He
told me of your pleasant party, and how
much he admired and regarded you both,

but not half as much about you as I want
to know ; indeed, how could he, when my
love for you makes me wish to trace your
every word and deed throughout the year.
He gave me your letter, and told us about
all the great personages now with you ;
but what was my grief to receive only one
music-box ! the box I prized — the one you
and Mary gave me — was missing ! I will
hope, however, that it was left with you,
and I shall still hear it in these deep
shades.

Your inquiries after your uncle, and how
we pass our time, can be more accurately
answered. My days are devoted to nursing and comforting my sick patient, who
walks only from the bed in which he break-
fasts to another, in the little room in which
you left him ; he is a little better, but not
well enough to get into a carriage to drive
to the Springs, which I fondly hoped he
might do. I expect Mrs. Randolph, Sep-
timia, and two Misses Jefferson Randolph
to-morrow, to pass a few days. My love
to Dolly and Richard, and accept my apology for this scrawl.

Your own and always,
DOLLY P. MADISON.

TO MARY.

MONTPELIER, *October* 31, 1835.

I was delighted to receive your last letter, my dearest Mary, as I am always, and sorry for your disappointment at not seeing Thomas and his wife. You inquire if Count d'Orsay has been here? Yes, he spent nearly three weeks with us, off and on, and seemed to enjoy himself very much. He is a great sportsman, and would borrow Payne's summer clothes, and go forth, returning as ragged as bushes and mire could make him, rest for several days, and then off again, tumbling into the river, losing his way — and yet come home laughing at his adventures. We found him an elegant young man, sensible and well-informed, except on the intricacies of our woods. I forget, now, who introduced him ; I think General Dearborn sent a letter of introduction. Mr. and Mrs. Stevenson stayed a week with me, but I have not yet heard from Mrs. Grimes and her children, of their time for coming. I must tell you that my English beauty has given me a calf as pretty as herself ; tell this to dear Dolly that she may be glad with me.

Have you any amusing books, no matter
how old, to lend me? You see in what
haste I write; tell me everything that you
are doing, dear girls; my heart follows you
all the time, in spite of my engrossing
family. It is now late at night, and my
eyes close. Dear love to you all. Good-
night, and sweet dreams! Your aunt

DOLLY.

TO JAMES MADISON.

By Edward Everett.

Happy the sage whose active race is run,
His warfare ended, and his labor done.
Him Heaven assigns, ere yet he's called away,
The peaceful evening of an honored day.
For him youth's eager appetite is o'er,
Which, ever nourished, asks for something
        more.
No more ambitious tasks, each toilsome hour,
To gain some loftier eminence of power.
Nor friends, nor party, now his strength con-
        trol,
And press a nation's troubles on his soul.
To him the sweets of life alone remain,
Without its care, its labor, and its pain.
Long may they thus remain, and late the day
When that strong sun shall shed its parting
        ray.

Warm, bright, and genial, was its morning
    hour,
And high and brilliant was its noon of power.
Long may its evening beams serenely shine,
While grateful millions bless its slow decline ;
Till gracious Heaven again shall bid it rise,
And shine to set no more, in purer skies.

    March 21, 1830.

CHAPTER XII.

As Mr. Madison grew weaker, and more crippled from rheumatism, they were obliged in a measure to close their hospitable doors. Mrs. Madison's whole time and thoughts were given to the invalid, and she writes to an old friend.: " I never leave my husband more than a few minutes at a time, and have not left the inclosure around my house for eight months, on account of his continued indisposition, of which friends at a distance have received but too favorable reports. Our physicians have advised the Warm Springs, and we hoped to have taken him there; but as he could not travel unless conveyed in his bed, we dare not think of it, at present. I can only express the hope, dearest friend, that my husband will be well enough for us to have the gratification of seeing you here before the winter throws it barriers between us. Nothing could give me more pleasure than to welcome you, and your daughter. Independently of my own feelings, I must ever love the kind friends of my dear sister."

At eighty-five years of age, though much reduced by disease and weakness, Mr. Madison's mind was bright, and his memory good. Though a great sufferer, he rarely complained, and his conversation was interesting and even lively until the last few days of illness.

The physicians were anxious to prolong his life until the Fourth of July, but he refused to take the necessary stimulants, and died June 28, 1836, in the full possession of all his faculties ; as serene, calm, and philosophical in his last moments, as he had been in all the trying occasions of life.

Governor James Barbour, a warm friend and neighbor, gives a touching description of his burial, where friends of all classes, from far and near, flocked to do honor to his memory, and the hundred slaves, as they turned to leave the newly-made grave, could control themselves no longer, and gave vent to their lamentations in one violent burst of grief that rent the air.

When at last the great bereavement and separation came upon Mrs. Madison, she did not dare give way to her grief. The feeling that there was something still to do for him, something that required all her energies, kept her up for several months, until the nervous strain produced its consequences, and her health gave way so completely, that during the following autumn and winter she was confined almost entirely to her bed. Left sole executrix, and with the responsibility of the unpublished manuscript her husband had worked upon so long and so faithfully in her hands, hundreds of letters and resolutions coming in from every side, expressive of grief and sympathy, there was no time to give way to her sense of utter loneliness in a separation from one with whom she had lived so happily for forty years. The replies were all written by herself, and one of the first was addressed to General Jackson, then President of the United States, who inclosed, with his own letter of condolence, the Resolutions of Congress on the death of Mr. Madison.

TO GENERAL JACKSON.

MONTPELIER, *July* 10, 1836.

I received, dear sir, in due time the communication from Congress, made more grateful to me by the kind sympathy which accompanied it.

The high and just estimation of my husband by my countrymen and friends, and their generous participation in the sorrow occasioned by our irretrievable loss, expressed through its supreme authorities and otherwise, is the only solace of which my heart is susceptible on the departure of him, who had never lost sight of that consistency, symmetry, and beauty of character in all its parts, which rendered his own transcendent as a whole and worthy of the best aspirations.

I am now preparing to execute the trust his confidence reposed in me, that of placing before Congress and the world what his pen had prepared for their use, and with the importance of this legacy, I am deeply impressed.

With great respect and friendship,

DOLLY P. MADISON.

TO RICHARD CUTTS, ESQ.

MONTPELIER, *July* 5, 1836.

I could never doubt your sympathy, dear brother, and require it much now. When can you come and see me? I hope it will be soon, relying on that hearty welcome always in store for you, and each one of your dear children, who have been even as my own. I wish you would see Mr. Morris at the Highlands, and say to him from me that his friendship is a dear consolation. I prize his advice, and, as from my early and most faithful friend, will strive to follow that contained in his letter of the 1st as well as any other which he may extend to me when he visits Montpelier. . . . I would write more, dear Richard, but have no power over my confused and oppressed mind to speak fully of the enduring goodness of my beloved husband. He left me many pledges of his confidence and love; especially do I value all his writings. From the proceeds of the first part of the "Debates in the Convention," I have to pay donations to several institutions. My brother and son are making a copy to send to England. Adieu, with love,

DOLLY P. MADISON.

When Congress assembled the following winter President Jackson sent a special message, proposing the purchase of Mr. Madison's manuscript, comprising a record of the Debates in the Congress of the Convention during the years 1782–1787. This manuscript was accepted as a national work, and thirty thousand dollars paid for it. A subsequent act was passed giving to Mrs. Madison the honorary privilege of a copyright in foreign countries, and later on Congress bestowed the franking privilege upon her, and voted her a seat upon the floors of the Senate and House, the only lady to whom such a distinction was ever given.

In 1837 the physicians persuaded her to try change of air and scene by a few weeks at the White Sulphur Springs, which had a very beneficial effect, and on her return she writes to her old friend, Mr. Anthony Morris: —

TO MR. ANTHONY MORRIS.

MONTPELIER, *September* 2, 1837.

Accept a thousand thanks, dear friend, for your two unanswered letters, containing the best advice in the world, and which

I have followed as far as I could on my visit to the White Sulphur Springs, a new world to me, who have never left Montpelier for nearly six years, even for a day. I passed three or four days at the Warm Springs, and two weeks at the White Sulphur, drinking moderately of the waters, and bathing my poor eyes a dozen times a day. The effect was excellent. My health was strengthened to its former standing, and my eyes grew white again ; but in my drive home of six days in the dust they took the fancy to relapse a little; still I cannot refrain from expressing with my own pen (forbidden by you) my grateful sense of your kind friendship on every occasion.

I met with many relations and friends on " my grand tour," and had every reason to be gratified, but for my own sad, impatient spirit, which continually dwelt on my duties at home yet unfinished. In truth, my five weeks' absence from Montpelier made me feel as if I had deserted my duties, and therefore was not entitled to the kindness everywhere shown me, and so I am at home at work again.

As winter approached and Mrs. Madison was left alone with her niece, Anna Payne, the daughter of a brother living in Kentucky, the memories and associations of the place became intolerable to her, and she made up her mind to spend the winter months, which for the first time she found desolate and dreary in the country, among her friends in Washington. A house on the corner of Lafayette Square and H Street, built by her brother-in-law, Richard Cutts, now belonged to her, and there she lived, enjoying the constant companionship of her nephews and nieces, every winter until her death.

As the time of mourning passed, her house again became filled with friends, and she was gladly welcomed back, receiving almost as much attention as she had done years before. On the 1st of January, the Fourth of July, and every other gala day, her house was thrown open, and the throng of visitors was equal to that which assembled at the White House. Friends and strangers of all grades came, many of them bringing their children and grandchildren, sure of the individual interest she took in them. On these occasions, as she became older, her memory sometimes played her false, but so gracefully was the mistake concealed or obviated that no one left her without the most agreeable impressions.

In 1844 Mrs. Madison was on board the ill-fated steamer Princeton, when the great cannon, called " the Peacemaker," exploded, and caused such terrible destruction of life. She was sitting below with some ladies, after dinner, when the crash came, followed by heart-rending shrieks, as one person after another was discovered to be injured. With great presence of mind she went about doing her best to soothe and assist in caring for the wounded, until forced to go home; there she found her drawing-room filled with anxious friends, waiting to be assured of her safety. She came in quietly, bowing gracefully and smiling, but unable to speak a word, with her heart full of sympathy for the sufferers she had just left ; nor could she ever afterwards trust herself to speak of that terrible afternoon, and she never heard it mentioned without turning pale and shuddering.

Her husband's judgment and care were

especially missed by Mrs. Madison with regard to her pecuniary affairs; accustomed to the most lavish hospitality, she was now, as she said, "too old to change her habits," and with an expensive plantation to keep up, which for some time brought in no returns owing to bad crops, and an extravagant, idle son, who, having spent his own fortune, lived upon her failing resources, she was in her old age obliged to sell the dearly-loved Montpelier, together with the slaves, to Mr. Moncure, of Richmond.

Most of the precious souvenirs were removed to "Toddsbirth," the residence of her son, Payne Todd, and here he intended his mother to pass the remaining years of her life; spending much money in carrying out his eccentric ideas for her comfort. The large house had been burned down, and several smaller ones were erected around a tower-like building, containing the ball-room and dining-room.

One of these cottages was to be for his mother, which, in order to obviate the fatigue of a staircase, she was to enter from the dining-room by a window. She never lived to see the completion of this plan, money becoming very scarce, and was always ready with excuses for her son. " My poor boy," she would say ; " forgive his eccentricities, for his heart is all right." And at another time would make use of Mr. Madison's favorite quotation : —

" Errors like straws upon the surface flow,
  Those who would seek for pearls must dive below."

Mrs. Madison always attended St. John's Episcopal Church in after life, while Mr. Hawley was the rector, and was baptized and confirmed there. In writing to her nephew she says : —

"And now, my dear Richard, I must tell you on what our thoughts have dwelt a great deal — and that is to become worthy of membership in the church which I have attended for the last forty years, and which Anna has attended all her life. Yesterday this long-wished-for confirmation took place. Bishop Whittingham performed the ceremony, and we had an excellent sermon from the Bishop of New Jersey — a fine preacher and beautiful champion for Charity which ' suspects not nor thinks no evil.' "

About this time she had a most providential escape from a fire, started by incendiaries, who placed matches between the shutters of the hall window and the staircase of her house. As the flames began to ascend towards her room in the early morning, a neighbor aroused the servants, and the man, Ralph, rushing towards his mistress' room, broke down the door and found her quietly sleeping in the midst of dense clouds of smoke. "Mistress," he cried, " I have come to save you," and awakening to the consciousness of danger to her husband's letters and papers, as more important than her own life, she refused to leave until the frightened servants secured them ; then Ralph seized her in his arms, rushed down the burning staircase, out of a side door, and placed her in safety in a remote corner of the garden. The fire was soon extinguished by kind neighbors, and Mrs. Madison laughingly returned, clad in a black velvet gown and nightcap, and with bare feet.

In 1846, Congress bought the remaining letters and private correspondence of Mr. Madison, together with those of Mr. Jefferson and Mr. Hamilton, paying twenty-five thousand dollars in each case.

During the eighty-second and last year of Mrs. Madison's life, her mind seemed very busy with the past. She caused old letters to be read to her, which brought in their train memories and associations unknown to those around her, and though her mind was never clouded, nor her affections weakened, she suffered much from debility and was confused and wearied by the conflicting counsels around her. "Oh, for my counselor!" she was heard to say, as if the burden of life was becoming too much for the tired brain. A few days before her death she said to a niece who had gone to her, as usual, for sympathy over some small grievance : —

" My dear, do not trouble about it ; there is nothing in *this* world worth really caring for. Yes," she repeated, looking intently out of a window, "believe me, I, who have lived so long, repeat to you there is nothing in this world here below worth caring for." These last days she was very fond of having the Bible read to her, and invariably asked for the Gospel of St. John, and it was at one of these times that her last sleep came upon her, sleep so profound that doctors were summoned and pronounced it slow apoplexy. For two days she lingered apparently without suffering, waking only when aroused to momentary consciousness, when she would smile lovingly, and put out her arms to embrace those whom she loved so well. Several times she murmured " My poor boy ! " as she seemed to feel her son's presence near her, and gently relapsed into that long rest which is peace.

Her funeral took place from St. John's Church, in Washington, and her remains were eventually deposited in the cemetery at Montpelier, near the monument erected over the grave of her illustrious husband.

Two years afterwards Payne Todd died from typhoid fever, attended by his mother's faithful servants, and full of grief for a wasted life.